CAREER SKILLS LIBRARY

Leadership
Skills

THIRD EDITION

CAREER SKILLS LIBRARY

Communication Skills

Finding A Job

Leadership Skills

Learning the Ropes

Organization Skills

Problem Solving

Professional Ethics and Etiquette

Research and Information Management

Teamwork Skills

FERGUSON

CAREER SKILLS LIBRARY

Leadership Skills

THIRD EDITION

Ferguson Publishing
An imprint of Infobase Publishing

Leadership Skills, Third Edition

Copyright © 1998, 2004, 2009 by Infobase Publishing

Ferguson
An imprint of Infobase Publishing
132 West 31st Street
New York NY 10001

Library of Congress Cataloging-in-Publication Data

Leadership skills. — 3rd ed.
   p. cm. — (Career skills library)
  Includes bibliographical references and index.
  ISBN-13: 978-0-8160-7776-2 (hardcover : alk. paper)
  ISBN-10: 0-8160-7776-2 (hardcover : alk. paper) 1. Leadership. 2.
Management. 3. Teams in the workplace. 4. Vocational guidance. I.
Ferguson Publishing.
  HD57.7.R686 2009
  658.4'092—dc22
                              2009007470

Text design by David Strelecky, adapted by Erik Lindstrom
Cover design by Takeshi Takahashi
First edition by Joe Mackall

Printed in the United States of America

MP ML 10 9 8 7 6 5 4 3 2 1

This book is printed on acid-free paper.

CONTENTS

INTRODUCTION

When we think of leaders, we may think of people such as Abraham Lincoln, Susan B. Anthony, or Martin Luther King, Jr. If you consider the historical importance and far-reaching influence of these individuals, leadership might seem like a noble but lofty goal. But like all of us, these people started out as students, workers, and citizens who possessed ideas about how some aspect of daily life could be improved on a larger scale. Through diligence and experience, they improved upon their ideas by sharing them with others, seeking their opinions and feedback, and constantly looking for the best way to accomplish goals for a group. Thus we all have the potential to be leaders at school, in our communities, and at work, regardless of age or experience. Leaders are vital at every level of an organization; cultivating leadership skills early is a great way to pave the way for success.

Many people have no desire to be leaders; after all, leadership comes with many responsibilities and risks that other members of a team do not have to worry about. Thus some people are more comfortable in the role of contributor. However, in much of today's world, teamwork is essential for completing projects and assignments, and teams without leaders usually are ineffective in achieving their goals. They flounder without a leader's help to focus on the goal and to make choices that will move the team toward that goal.

In school and extracurricular activities, you may be able to avoid the responsibilities of leadership: Someone else usually will step forward to take on a leadership role. But in the workplace, the choice will not always be yours. When you are assigned a project, you will most likely need to rely on the help and support of others. These people, in effect, become your team. To get the most out of their efforts, you will need to exercise good leadership.

Leaders inspire others to act by setting good examples. Their drive and perseverance spur others on. Leaders strive to be the best they can be—not to compete with others. In fact, a leader's job is to help others make their best contribution toward a shared goal.

Leaders motivate others through mutual trust. The leader must trust in his or her teammates' abilities and willingness to pursue a goal. At the same time, the team must trust in their leader's ability and willingness to provide needed support. This mutual trust is essential in building a team that will be successful in reaching its goal.

Martin Luther King, Jr. was a charismatic leader and civil rights activist. However, leaders are found not just in activism; they are needed in all areas of business and society. (AP Photo)

DID YOU KNOW?

A leader's job is to help others make their best contribution toward a shared goal.

Seventy-three percent of employers surveyed by The Conference Board in 2006 rated high school graduates as deficient in leadership skills.

Source: *Are They Really Ready to Work?*

In today's workplace, you need to develop leadership skills to build and direct teams to get work done. Although some leadership qualities are inborn, many of the skills necessary for good leadership can be learned. In this book, we discuss ways of interacting with others that will help you lead them to success. Topics include:

- Motivating others
- Giving and taking criticism
- Organizing a project
- Delegating responsibility
- Monitoring a team's progress
- Learning leadership skills on the job

Leadership is inspiring others to follow your vision/ direction/dream. In business, this means getting people aligned and moving in one direction—the direction that makes the business fly.

—Steve Robbins, motivational speaker and entrepreneur

This book covers the following leadership topics:

- The basic characteristics of a leader
- The importance of leadership when working with others as a team
- Giving and receiving criticism
- How leaders set goals and motivate others
- Organizational tools that help leaders delegate and teams to stay focused
- Completing projects through effective leadership and team building
- How to cultivate leadership qualities

1

LEADERSHIP— WHAT IT IS AND WHY IT MATTERS

"Peter, I need you to prepare a report on our company's services for a prospective new client," says his boss. "We've been trying to get their business for more than a year. You've got decent graphic design skills, so make the report look good."

Although Peter started working only four months ago, he hopes to become an assistant manager as soon as a position becomes available. He is glad he took a desktop publishing course last summer. The skills he learned there might help him get the promotion he's been waiting for.

Peter has been frustrated that his efforts at work up to this point have not been recognized by his supervisor. Peter always gets to work early, stays late, and often works through lunch. He's proud that he is usually able to finish his assignments well before they are due. He looks down on his coworkers who seem content

✔ TRUE OR FALSE?

Do You Know the Qualities of a Good Leader?

1. Good leaders are conservative when making decisions.

2. I will only be successful as a manager if I have a college degree.

3. The top-down leadership style is the only effective management style.

4. Strong leaders are always consistent.

Test yourself as you read through this chapter. The answers appear on pages 37–38.

to take all the allotted time to complete their work. It doesn't bother him that not one of his coworkers even says hello anymore, but he deeply cares that no one in management seems to notice his hard work. This new client report may finally get their attention.

Peter knows he will need help from his fellow staff members to complete the report. Fortunately, he can make them put aside their individual projects to supply him with what he needs to do his report. When one clerk seems deliberately slow in finding a file Peter needs, a reminder that the boss has put Peter in charge is all it takes.

Since he prides himself on finishing every project early, he tells the staff that the report is due in three days, instead of the actual deadline the following

THE BENEFITS OF LEADERSHIP

According to the Center for Creative Leadership, companies that spend money developing leaders "improve [their] bottom-line financial performance, attract and retain talent, drive a performance culture, and increase organizational agility."

week. "I'm the only one who cares," he thinks, as his coworkers grumble about working late two nights in a row.

Peter is glad that his boss finally seems to be aware of how hard he works. He smiles to himself when he notices his boss watching him more and more. Since Peter is a perfectionist, he naturally checks and rechecks every detail anyway; having his boss see him in action is just a well-deserved bonus.

When the report is finished, Peter knows that he has done an excellent job. "This will really do it," he thinks. Later his boss says the report is a "thorough, competent effort." Peter is disappointed. He had expected higher praise. He is also disappointed a few weeks later with his six-month review. His supervisor has given him low ratings in the categories "leadership" and "potential for promotion."

"I stand on my head and it's not enough," he thinks. "I'm smarter than most of the managers, and I work harder. What's it going to take to convince them?"

QUALITIES OF A LEADER

Although there are different styles of leadership, all effective leaders share certain characteristics. These are qualities that can be learned and improved upon over time.

Innovative and Confident

Leaders must be able to do the job, but ability alone is not enough. True leadership requires a willingness to be bold, to consider unusual approaches to problems, to do more than just follow tried-and-true methods. Leaders are self-confident and have no need to put others down to feel good about themselves. They are willing to stand up for their ideas and debate them with others. This kind of intellectual competition is characteristic of a good leader. In *Planning for Nonplanners,* Darryl Ellis and Peter Pekar, Jr. call this characteristic "constructively competitive." They also note that exceptional leaders know how to be competitive without alienating others.

Exceptional leaders know how to be competitive without alienating others.

Respectful of Others

Balancing competition with respect may be difficult for young employees who think the way to get ahead is to outshine their coworkers. But neither workers nor supervisors like or respect leaders who think only of themselves. The staff of Catalyst, a national nonprofit organization devoted to career advancement for women, suggests keeping a low profile while you are new on the job. In *Making the Most of Your First Job,* the Catalyst staff notes that if you're too "gung ho" at first, people will resent you. Resentful coworkers will certainly not be motivated to cooperate with you.

Today's market is competitive and volatile. To be successful, our business needs to be dynamic and ahead of our competitors. In order to accomplish this we need strong leaders within every business unit driving innovation and efficiency. Having leaders with focus, motivation, and the ability to drive change throughout our workplace will allow us to accomplish our goals.

—Molly McKenna, director, GSI Education & Training, Thomson Reuters

Above all, leadership requires the ability to get along with others in a variety of situations. For example, if you are class president, you won't be able to accomplish much if you begin to think too highly of yourself. Classmates you snub are not likely to volunteer to help with prom decorations. Likewise, if you are an assistant manager and ignore your coworkers until you need something, you will not always get the results you want.

LEADERS ARE . . .

- Team players
- Sensitive
- Creative
- Confident
- Fond of people
- Street smart
- Organized
- Trustworthy
- Communicators

Ethical

If you pay attention to the news, you have probably noticed the ethics scandals in the accounting and financial services industries, as well as at all governmental levels. These scandals have cost the American people billions of dollars and have caused many to lose confidence in business and government leaders.

What are ethics? Ethics are a code of rules about how we act toward others. They deal with right and wrong.

It is extremely important that you act ethically in all aspects of your life—at home, school, and at work—especially if you are a manager. As a manager, you set the tone for your entire company. Your employees will constantly be observing your words and actions, so it is key that you act ethically in every instance. Be sure that you understand your organization's ethics policies and have the conviction to uphold them.

Courteous

In *Why Employees Don't Do What They're Supposed to Do and What to Do About It,* Ferdinand F. Fournies reminds managers to treat their staff members with such common courtesies as saying "please" and "thank you," apologizing for being late to a meeting, and not interrupting people while they are speaking. Other leaders in business and industry recommend the golden rule: Treat others as you would like to be treated.

The workplace is still primarily a place where people interact. The social skills we have been practicing all our lives are important in business, too. Fournies tells managers to look at people's faces when they are talking, to avoid sarcastic comments, and to control emotional outbursts. Sarcasm and temper tantrums are not acceptable in a social setting and even less so in the workplace. Being in a supervisory position doesn't give you the right to be discourteous.

DID YOU KNOW?

- According to a survey of MBA programs by the World Resources Institute and

The Aspen Institute, 54 percent of MBA programs require students to take one or more courses in ethics, sustainability, corporate social responsibility, or business and society—an increase of 20 percent since 2001.

- In an effort to create more ethical graduates, colleges are asking graduating students to make the following pledge: "I, _____, pledge to explore and take into account the social and environmental consequences of any job I consider and will try to improve these aspects of any organizations for which I work." The pledge has been introduced at more than 100 colleges and universities including Berea College, Cornell University, and the University of Wisconsin-Madison. Visit http://www.graduationpledge.org/new for more information.

- Junior Achievement is a nonprofit organization that teaches young people about business issues. It hosts an annual essay contest to encourage teens to think about ethical issues. The winner receives a $5,000 college scholarship. Visit http://studentcenter.ja.org/aspx/ LearnEthics/ethics_essay_rules.aspx for more information.

- The Gallup Organization recently asked a group of 1,009 adults to name the most ethical careers. The winners (in descending order): nurses, pharmacists, veterinarians, physicians, dentists, engineers, college teachers, clergy, and police officers.

Sensitive

Good leaders must also be sensitive to the feelings and needs of others. These needs are not always clearly expressed. Sometimes people do not even know what they want or need. Talented leaders are able to "read" the people around them and adjust their own behavior accordingly.

Alissa, a college student and part-time office manager for a local nonprofit organization, says the hardest part of her job is figuring out her coworkers. "When Ellie drags her feet on an assignment, it probably means she doesn't feel capable of doing it. Maybe I'll need to give her some more help. When Jerry forgets I asked him to do something, it might mean I've been pushing him too hard—I do rely on him a lot because we're such a small staff."

Alissa has already learned to pick up on her coworkers' cues and act accordingly. Her sensitivity and support motivate her staff and make her an effective leader.

Another aspect of being sensitive is having the ability to listen to your employees. Listening is a

✍ EXERCISE

- Previously in this chapter, we learned about how insensitive Peter is to his coworkers and his supervisor. Reread the story and find three mistakes Peter makes. Then explain how he can change his behavior to become a more effective leader.

- Have you ever served in a leadership position in a school club? If so, what type of leadership style did you use? Was it successful? If given another chance, what would you change about the way you lead others?

- Are you a natural leader? Write down 5–7 of your best qualities (such as confident, organized, etc.) on a piece of paper, then look at the list of necessary qualities for successful leaders on page 12. Does your list match up with that list? If not, try improve yourself by incorporating some of these qualities into your life.

workplace skill that is often overlooked, but according to Dr. David Wolf, a life skills coach, workers use their listening skills three times as often as their speaking skills. Listening closely to your employees will provide you with valuable information "from the trenches" regarding the status of projects. It will also help you to get to know your employees better and build a rapport with them.

Good listening skills are especially important when an employee comes to you with bad news. Your first instinct might be to interrupt your employee (or perhaps even get angry) as he or she details the problem. But it's important to keep your cool and refrain from responding until you've heard the complete report. Dr. Wolf says that "one of the keys to effective listening is to separate your emotions from the speaker's emotions or problem." Doing this will help you to remain calm and formulate an effective solution to the problem.

GOING BEYOND ABILITY

Paul has been a member of the high-school Key Club, a service organization, for three years. He decided to ask his friend Scott, the current president, to nominate him to be next year's president. "I think I deserve it," Paul thought. "I never miss a meeting and I'm willing to do anything they ask me. I've helped at every car wash, distributed turkeys at Thanksgiving, and even volunteered at the senior citizen center every Tuesday this past year. And I know I'd be better than anybody else at keeping track of the money we raise for charity."

Paul certainly has contributed much to the Key Club. He has always been a conscientious and capable worker. But Scott was hesitant to promise to nominate

Paul. Scott decided to speak to the club adviser about his worries.

☛ FACT

Leaders need to work through others to be successful. About 50–60 percent of leaders fail because they are unable to build and guide an effective team.

"This has been a harder job than I thought it would be. Running the meetings and keeping everybody interested in our long-term projects was tough. Sometimes I felt like being a drill-sergeant, but I knew that wouldn't work. I had to figure out ways to make the members take responsibility without being too harsh," Scott told his adviser. "Paul is not really a people person—I just don't think he's right for this position."

The adviser agreed. She and Scott decided to ask Paul if he would be interested in running for the office of club treasurer. Although Paul was disappointed, he was also secretly relieved. "Maybe I'd just better stick to what I'm good at," he thought.

Paul's story shows that although experience and ability are important leadership qualities, they must be balanced with courteousness, respect for others, and sensitivity. A good leader possesses much more than skill. Although this isn't the right time for Paul to take on the leadership role of club president, this experience may help him develop these skills for future leadership positions.

FUTURE SKILLS FOR SUCCESS

In 2007, the Center for Creative Leadership asked business leaders to name three skills that they believed future leaders would need to be successful. Their responses indicate that future leaders will need to have strong skills in team-building, relationship-building, collaboration, and change management (the ability to oversee companies in changing markets and in other demanding circumstances). Here is the complete list (ranked in order of importance).

1. Collaboration
2. Change leadership
3. Building effective teams
4. Influence without authority
5. Driving innovation
6. Coaching
7. Building and mending relationships
8. Adaptability
9. Seeing things from different angles
10. Learning from others through questions
11. Resourcefulness
12. Leveraging differences

13. Global awareness

14. Decisiveness

15. Doing whatever it takes to get results

16. Straightforwardness/composure

17. Credibility

18. Ethical decision-making

A DEGREE IS NO GUARANTEE OF SUCCESS

People often think they are good at something because they have done well in a school setting. But a good grade, a diploma, or even a college degree is no guarantee of success in the workplace. In fact, the brilliant student is often *too* smart for his or her own good. This student may think no one can teach him or her anything and, as a result, cannot learn.

With surprising frequency, individuals who were academic superstars in high school, college, and even business school have dramatically less success in their managerial careers.

—Richard K. Wagner and Robert J. Sternberg in *Measures of Leadership*

Robert Sternberg and Richard Wagner's research reveals that academic leaders are often not as successful when they start out in the workplace; they

MOST COMMON UNDERGRADUATE DEGREES FOR CEOS

Chief executive officers employed by S&P 500 companies in 2008 had a variety of academic backgrounds, and only 10 percent earned their degrees from an Ivy League institution. Here are the most popular undergraduate majors for CEOs:

- Engineering: 22 percent

- Economics: 16 percent

- Business Administration: 13 percent

- Accounting: 9 percent

- Liberal Arts: 6 percent

sometimes lack the practical knowledge or "street smarts" it takes to be a leader at work. This doesn't mean they will never get ahead. They may just need some time to learn the ropes.

The staff of Catalyst, in *Making the Most of Your First Job,* gives this advice: "In an office environment, everyday experience rates higher than a genius IQ. Unlike a mathematical equation, office problems aren't always clear-cut. Perhaps you don't have all the information you need to understand, let alone solve,

Asking others for their opinions will not make you seem less capable.

the problem. Or perhaps there will be several solutions to your problem. Only practical, on-the-job experience can help you accurately weigh your options and make the best choice for your company."

People who have been on the job longer than you can be a great help. Asking others for their opinions will not make you seem less capable. In fact, it indicates a willingness to learn. And it does not matter if the experienced worker is lower than you in the company. It is their experience that counts.

Another kind of knowledge that you can pick up on the job only is the company's *unwritten rules.* One executive in the Wagner and Sternberg study describes this as knowing "what goes without saying." New employees need to keep their eyes and ears open and be cautious about saying too much too soon. Other unwritten rules might include not using the executive elevator, refraining from playing music loudly (or at all) if you work in a cubicle, or being required to treat the office to cookies or cake on your birthday.

✍ EXERCISE

Describe a time you were the "new kid on the block." Was there something you did or said that you now realize was a mistake? What could you have done differently?

LEADERSHIP STYLES

When Richard was chosen to direct a long-term project at the firm where he worked, his coworkers were delighted. Richard's projects usually went well. Everybody always ended up feeling good about his or her work.

While his bosses valued Richard's initiative and creative thinking, his staff more often praised his flexibility and openness to suggestions. These qualities make his staff feel that they have something to contribute. In fact, Richard's attitude encourages them to be creative and take initiative.

"At meetings, I feel safe speaking my mind," says one coworker.

"We don't always have to do everything his way," says another.

"I'm interested in what my staff thinks," says Richard. "Their input is important to me. I don't believe in the top-down style of management; good ideas can come from anywhere."

Some leaders are comfortable with employee participation in problem solving. Like Richard, they feel there is a lot to be gained through listening to many opinions. Others manage employees with a more directive style. Sometimes the style will depend on the type of project or on the individuals included in the work team. A top-down style might be best for a complicated project with many parts or for a team whose members are mostly new or entry-level employees. But usually a leader's style is just that—his or her style.

LEARN MORE ABOUT IT: LEADERSHIP STYLES

Books

Harvey, Andrew J., and Raymond E. Foster. *Leadership: Texas Hold 'Em Style*. Charleston, S.C.: BookSurge, 2007.

Jackson, John, and Lorraine Bosse-Smith. *Leveraging Your Leadership Style: Maximize Your Influence by Discovering the Leader Within*. Nashville, Tenn.: Abingdon Press, 2008.

Potter, Ronald, and Wayne Hastings. *Trust Me: Developing a Leadership Style People Will Follow*. Charleston, S.C.: BookSurge, 2008.

Web Sites

Leadership Styles
    http://www.nwlink.com/~donclark/leader/leadstl.
    html

Mind Tools: Leadership Styles
    http://www.mindtools.com/pages/article/
    newLDR_84.htm

Motivation and Leadership Styles
    http://www.motivation-tools.com/workplace/
    leadership_styles.htm

LEADERSHIP STYLE SURVEY QUIZ

Visit http://www.nwlink.com/~donclark/ leader/survstyl.html to take a short quiz to help you determine your leadership style.

Having a leadership style makes things easier for your employees. They come to know what to expect. If you usually welcome their ideas, they won't expect you to jump on a staff member who has a suggestion. On the other hand, if you usually give a lot of exact instructions for performing an assignment, your staff has probably come to depend on that. They will be uncomfortable if you tell them to "do whatever you think is best." A consistent approach helps build trust.

Here are a few of the most popular leadership styles:

Authoritarian/Autocratic. Authoritarian leaders have a clear idea of what should be done, how a task should be done, and when it should be completed and rarely, if ever, ask employees for input. Until recent years, this was the predominant leadership style. Researchers have found that employees who work under this type of manager are less creative, more likely to be absent from work, and more likely to leave their jobs.

Steve Jobs, cofounder, chairman, and CEO of Apple Inc., has a charismatic leadership style. (Paul Sakuma, AP Photo)

Participative/Democratic. Unlike the authoritarian style, participative leaders provide instruction to employees, but encourage them to provide suggestions on how work on a project could be improved. They are good communicators and are happy to pitch in and help with group assignments to encourage team spirit. A study has found that participative leadership is the most effective leadership style. Employees who work for a manager who uses this style typically produce high quality, high quantity work.

Delegative/Free Reign. Delegative leaders let group members make most or all decisions and provide little or no guidance. This approach should only be used with trusted workers who are highly skilled and able to work without much oversight.

Charismatic. Charismatic leaders use energetic encouragement to inspire their teams. They are often ego-driven, believing that the main reason that their employees achieve is because of their leadership abilities. This belief is often translated to employees, who might come to believe a project can't be completed without their manager's oversight.

Tranformational. Transformational leaders are inspiring individuals who are able to get team members to buy into their vision of a project or, in the instance of a CEO, the future of a company. They are media savvy and excellent communicators, but they focus more on the big picture rather than details. They often delegate tasks and need a strong assistant to ensure that projects move along as expected.

Situational. Situational leaders combine one or more of the leadership styles listed above as needed based on the project requirements and the personalities they are working with.

BUILDING TRUST

People respond to leaders they can trust. They need to be able to count on their leader to do the right thing, whether it's in school, a club, or a job. For example, if you agree to be in charge of a committee, others are depending on you. They are willing to be workers, but you have accepted the responsibility

A consistent approach helps build trust.

🔊 EXERCISE

What type of leader do you prefer working with? Think about your experiences in the classroom, past summer or after-school jobs, or student clubs. Do you prefer working with leaders that ask for group input? Or do you prefer a leader who is a take-charge individual? What were the benefits or disadvantages to both types of leaders?

of leading them. If you let them down, you may lose their trust.

Raymond was in charge of the advertisers' program for the sports banquet. The members of his committee were to visit local businesses to ask them to support school sports by buying an ad in the program. Raymond had many volunteers for his committee because the money from the ads would benefit all the school's teams. Also, Raymond had promised the volunteers that he would provide them with lists of local stores that participated in the past.

Gary, last year's chairman, had given Raymond a folder to help get him started. It included copies of the programs from the last several years. Gary had also made notes about the best times to visit particular businesses and whom to speak with. When Raymond had mentioned this at the sports-council meeting, he really hooked a lot of volunteers.

"I usually hate soliciting donations and things," said Sandy, one of the volunteers. "But it makes a difference if you know whom to ask for, and that they've done it before."

Unfortunately, Raymond had misplaced the folder Gary had given him. "I'm sure it will turn up soon," he told himself. "I'll bring it in soon," he told everybody else. "I'm retyping it."

After looking at home and in his locker, Raymond began to think he had accidentally thrown the folder out. "If I tell the volunteers I don't have the information I promised, some of them might drop out. I'd better not say anything to anybody until the kick-off meeting. They wouldn't walk out on the meeting. We'll just have to use the phone book. I know some of the kids will be upset, but they'll just have to deal with it."

At the kick-off meeting a few days later, Raymond asked Sandy to go to the office to get a phone book. When Sandy realized that it was for making lists of businesses to contact, she felt cheated.

"I should never have volunteered," she thought. "And I never would have if I had known it would be like this."

Sandy was probably not the only one who felt that way. An unexpected or unexplained change in our situation makes us uncomfortable. Some people are able to rise to the challenge of new circumstances.

Others may not be able to. But in either case, like Sandy, they probably will feel cheated.

☛ FACT

According to a survey by management consulting firm Accenture, 50 percent of respondents rated leadership and management skills as the most important traits that enable workers to do their job better.

No one feels comfortable with a supervisor who tells Employee A one thing and Employee B another or a coworker who says one thing and does another. Why would anyone do this? The answer is usually office politics. Some people say or do whatever they think will help them get ahead. Dealing with these kinds of people is very difficult. We soon lose our trust and respect for them.

There are other ways people can lose our trust. You may recognize a friend, or even yourself, in some of the categories in "The Trust Busters" list that follows. But a leader who behaves in these ways will not be followed for long.

MAINTAINING BALANCE IN DEALING WITH OTHERS

Although no one likes a dictator, we do expect our leaders to exert their authority to keep things

WORKPLACE MORALE BUSTERS

Bosses have many expectations for their employees, but in order for a company to be successful managers also have a responsibility to treat their employees fairly. Failure to do so can adversely affect morale. OfficeTeam, a staffing service that specializes in highly skilled administrative professionals, asked workers to detail one action by their bosses that causes the most negative impact on their morale. Thirty-percent of respondents said that "lack of open, honest communication" was the biggest morale killer. "Consistently sharing good—and bad—news with staff members builds an atmosphere of trust and can forestall potential miscommunication on business issues," says Diane Domeyer, executive director of OfficeTeam.

Other morale busters included "failure to recognize employee achievements, micromanaging employees, and excessive workloads for extended periods."

running smoothly. When they do not, everyone suffers.

Meg is the assistant night manager for a clothing store in a mall. One of her salespeople, Chrissy, often has friends visit during the evening. Chrissy talks with her visitors while Meg and Donna, the other salesperson, scurry to help customers and straighten the shelves.

Although having visitors is against company policy, Meg is reluctant to say anything to Chrissy. "It's not worth the attitude she'll give me," Meg thinks. Meg already glares at Chrissy when her friends bring food into the store—prompting them to put it away in a hurry. "At least they're careful around the clothes," Meg thinks. "Is it worth fighting over a few crumbs on the floor?"

THE TRUST BUSTERS

- *The blabber* tells people everyone else's business. A person in a leadership position sometimes has access to private information. This does not give them the privilege of telling anyone else.

- *The manipulator* may only tell you what he or she wants you to know. This person uses deception or plays on people's fears or emotions to get desired information. This is controlling, not leading.

- *The exploiter* takes advantage of others. This person's position may give him or her power, but misusing it will cause resentment and resistance.

- *The stealer* always takes more than his or her share. This person takes more privileges

There is a lot to be done at closing time each evening. Meg has posted a list of duties on the wall behind the cash register. Chrissy always manages to take so long rehanging clothing that Donna is stuck with the vacuuming almost every night. The big commercial machine is really heavy, so vacuuming is everybody's least-favorite job. Night after night, Donna seethes as she pushes the awkward appliance around, especially whenever she finds crumbs on the carpet.

than other coworkers, taking the best assignments or taking credit for others' work and ideas.

- *The agree-er* is much more pleasant to be around. This person is always ready to give others a pat on the back. The problem is that others don't really know where they stand with the agree-er. A good leader must also be a teacher who helps others improve by providing an honest reaction.

- *The avoider* is also dishonest in his or her reactions. This person might say, "I'll think about it," because he or she doesn't want to say, "No." The avoider deals with unpleasant situations by simply avoiding them. This puts more pressure and responsibility on others.

CAREERS FOR LEADERS

Do you think you would make a good leader, but don't know what careers beyond CEO that require this important skill? If so, you should visit the Skills Search section of O*NET Online, a U.S. government resource for occupational information. By selecting at least one of 10 basic skills, complex problem solving skills, four resource management skills, six social skills, three system skills, and 11 technical skills, you can find careers that are a good match for your abilities. Some in-demand careers that require leadership skills include:

Advertising and promotions managers

Computer and information systems managers

Construction managers

Education administrators, elementary and secondary school

Education administrators, postsecondary

Education administrators, preschool and child care center/program

Financial managers, branch or department

First-line supervisors/ managers of personal service workers

First-line supervisors/ managers of police and detectives

Food service managers

Forest fire fighting and prevention supervisors

General and operations managers

Lodging managers

Medical and health services managers

Municipal fire fighting and prevention supervisors

Purchasing managers

Sales managers

Ship and boat captains

Treasurers and controllers

In fact, dozens of careers are listed, with information on job responsibilities and other necessary skills provided for each job. Visit http://online.onetcenter.org to use this useful career exploration tool.

✍ EXERCISE

It is not necessary to bite people's heads off to let them know you're in charge. A good leader can find a balance between being an ogre and a pushover. Describe how Meg might handle the two problems she has with Chrissy. (Make up a conversation between them if you want.)

Why doesn't Meg say anything to Chrissy? As the night manager, Meg certainly has the authority. But fearful of a conflict, Meg does nothing. Perhaps she hopes the problem will go away.

Generally, however, problems get worse when we don't deal with them. Nor is it fair to expect Donna and Chrissy to work it out themselves. This puts an unfair burden on Donna. It's the leader's job to resolve problems.

The leader must know, must know that he knows, and must be able to make it abundantly clear to those about him that he knows.

—Clarence Belden Randall, former spokesman and Chairman of Inland Steel Company

Those in charge sometimes worry that people won't like them if they use their authority. But followers won't like a leader who shirks his or her responsibility

READ MORE ABOUT IT: FAMOUS LEADERS

Karson, Jill. *Profiles in History: Leaders of the Civil Rights Movement.* Farmington Hills, Mich.: Greenhaven Press, 2004.

Lodge, Tom. *Mandela: A Critical Life.* New York: Oxford University Press, USA, 2007.

McCain, John, and Mark Salter. *Faith of My Fathers: A Family Memoir.* New York: Harper, 2008.

Obama, Barack. *Dreams from My Father: A Story of Race and Inheritance.* New York: Three Rivers Press, 2004.

Weigel, George. *Witness to Hope: The Biography of Pope John Paul II.* New York: Harper Perennial, 2005.

The key to great leadership is trust. A leader who does not earn trust will soon be without followers.

to take actions or make decisions that need to be made. Even in a participatory style of leadership, the leader must be the last one to make decisions. Letting things drift accomplishes nothing and makes everyone uncomfortable. If you've accepted a leadership role, you must be willing to take charge.

Being a leader is sometimes very difficult. Ability and hard work are not enough. Leadership requires skills in solving problems, sensitivity in dealing with others, and a willingness to make decisions and take action. But the key to great leadership is trust. A leader who does not earn trust will soon be without followers.

✔ TRUE OR FALSE: ANSWERS

Do You Know the Qualities of a Good Leader?

1. Good leaders are conservative when making decisions.

False. Successful leaders are bold and unafraid of making hard decisions. They are willing to try to new approaches if they can't solve a problem by using conventional methods.

2. I will only be successful as a manager if I have a college degree.

False. Successful managers have a variety of educational backgrounds—from high school diplomas to Ph.D.s. For example, Mark Begich, the mayor of Anchorage, Alaska from 2003 to 2009, never earned a college degree, but earned raves for his leadership of the city. In 2008, he was elected to the U.S. Senate.

3. The top-down leadership style is the only effective management style.

False. There are many types of leadership styles, and what works for a manager of 10 copywriters at an advertising firm may not work for an individual who oversees hundreds of different types of workers in a automotive manufacturing plant. The key is to find the management style that matches your personality and helps you to get things done in the workplace.

4. Strong leaders are always consistent.

True. Once you choose a management style, it's important to maintain this style to gain the confidence and trust of your employees. For example, if you are a very hands-on manager, then be hands-on in every situation. If you have led by using a hands-off approach, then trust your workers to do the job—even in times of stress.

IN SUMMARY . . .

- Leaders must be competitive, yet compassionate.

- Leaders must be able to work with others.

- Leaders need book smarts *and* street smarts.

- Different leadership styles work in different environments and situations.

- It is important to maintain trust between the leader and his or her workers.

- When necessary, leaders should be able to confront problems and people head on.

2

WORKING
WITH OTHERS

Felicia has worked part time in a gift shop for two years. Because of her experience, she feels knowledgeable about the business and very sure of herself. Mary, the owner, also has confidence in Felicia, relying on her more than the other part-time workers.

One Saturday, Mrs. Ellis, a frequent customer, purchased a silver tray for an anniversary present and requested that it be gift wrapped. Felicia carefully peeled off the price sticker before she wrapped the gift. After Mrs. Ellis had left, Janice, a fairly new sales clerk, quietly approached Felicia.

"I noticed that you threw the price sticker away. I'm so forgetful that I have to keep it where I can see it, or else I start to wonder if I really did remove it." Janice added, "In the last shop I worked at, we had to stick it on the store copy of the receipt. That way we could double-check just by glancing at the

✔ TRUE OR FALSE?

Do You Know How to Work with Others?

1. All types of criticism are wrong.

2. Fear is an excellent motivational tool for managers.

3. Training workers takes time and effort.

4. As a manager, it's important to monitor a worker's performance during a project.

Test yourself as you read through this chapter. The answers appear on pages 60–61.

receipt. Just thought I'd suggest it because it really helped me."

Felicia couldn't believe what she was hearing. "I've been working here for two years and I've never once forgotten to remove the tag when the item is to be wrapped," she retorted.

Janice was stunned. "Sorry. I was only trying to help."

A few months later, Mrs. Burton, a newlywed, asked for Felicia's help in selecting a birthday present. She told Felicia she had a limited budget but hoped to find something special for her new mother-in-law. Felicia asked several questions about the mother-in-law's tastes and finally recommended a crystal vase. Mrs. Burton was thrilled to find that it was on sale and that there was no charge for gift-wrapping. "I'll

THE BENEFITS OF CRITICISM

According to the International Women's Media Foundation, constructive criticism

- provides feedback that enhances job results

- leads to personal and professional development

- reduces stress and creates psychological security

- improves interpersonal relationships

- helps develop the ideal organizational climate

certainly be sure to come in here whenever I need a present," she said.

A few days later, Mrs. Burton returned and asked for Felicia again. "I can't begin to describe how upset I was when my mother-in-law opened my gift and found the price still on the bottom of the vase. I was so embarrassed. You really should be more careful in the future."

Felicia was mortified, especially because her boss Mary was close enough to hear the complaint. Mary came over and apologized along with Felicia, but both suspected that Mrs. Burton would not be back to shop again soon.

"Next time maybe I'll listen to what my coworkers have to say," thought Felicia. "I guess I don't know everything."

CONSTRUCTIVE CRITICISM

Being criticized is almost always unpleasant, whether it is done by your friends, family, coworkers, or superiors. The important thing to remember is that criticism is not an attack on you, it is feedback on something that you've done. Very often people offer criticism to encourage improvement, not to suggest that you lack ability. If you can separate who you are from what you do, you will not feel the need to strike back or be defensive when you receive criticism.

There's nothing dreadful about "being wrong"— everyone is at times. However, if you don't realize when you've made an error or if you stubbornly refused to accept it, you have fallen into an all-too-familiar snare.

—J. W. McLean and William Weitzel in
Leadership—Magic, Myth, or Method

Acknowledging a mistake will not make your coworkers think less of you—as long as you also take steps to correct it. The purpose of criticism is, after all, to help someone improve. Your peers are often in the best position to know your weaknesses as well as your strengths.

Be sure to listen when you receive criticism. Even if the criticism is not deserved, look for the kernel of truth that might be there. If you are able to consider what others want to tell you without being defensive, you have an opportunity to learn from them.

If you are a leader, it is especially important to listen to criticism, since the higher you move up the ladder the less criticism you will receive. Feedback from our peers, or even our subordinates, can show us where we need to improve.

Feedback from our peers, or even our subordinates, can show us where we need to improve.

CRITICISM FROM A SUPERIOR

No matter how high you go in an organization, it is likely that you will still have someone above you. Part of your supervisor's job is to advise you. Some of this advice may sting—criticism can indeed hurt. However, remember that your superior's intent is usually to teach and guide you. This guidance can only help you improve your performance and advance your career. So take it like a professional: don't interrupt, make excuses, or blame someone else.

This does not mean that you should say nothing at all. Your response should indicate that you understand the points being made (or question further if you do not) and accept that you need to make an improvement. Beth Collins, senior planner for a clothing retail chain, says that a simple "okay" is the worst response.

✍ EXERCISE

Constructive criticism can help us improve. Think of a time a teacher or other superior criticized your work. How did it help you improve your performance?

"The employer may think you are just giving lip service; that you hear, but not necessarily that you agree, or even understand," Collins says. "Your answer should show that you recognize that there is an issue that needs to be addressed. Ideally, I'd hope for a response that included how you plan to handle the same situation in the future."

THE DIFFICULTIES OF GIVING CRITICISM

Jason worked nights at a diner that was a popular gathering place for high school students. Jason knew many of the students because he had only graduated two years earlier. He now attended the local community college, but he hoped to transfer to a prestigious culinary college after completing his associate's degree the following year. He had always approached his job at the diner with a high degree of dedication and seriousness, and he had been rewarded for his efforts by a recent promotion to assistant manager.

One of Jason's new responsibilities was supervising the servers. He knew everything about their tasks because he had been a waiter before his promotion. But he still sometimes felt uncomfortable telling workers what to do.

Greg, a high school senior, had started working at the diner a few months ago. He was popular with the customers and his coworkers. His only fault was that he was occasionally late for his shift. One evening, Jason had to keep customers waiting because one waitress was out sick and Greg was late. Jason started feeling frantic and was just about to start taking the customers' orders when Greg walked in with several friends.

"Where have you been? Have you got a lot of nerve!" Jason yelled. "We're going crazy while you just take your sweet time getting here. You do this all the time lately and you're taking advantage of everybody else. You must think you're above the rules! Well, I'll tell you what I think," Jason added, "I think your attitude and your work stinks. You can't even fill the salt and pepper shakers without spilling. You'll never make it in this business."

When Jason calmed down, he realized he had overreacted. His own panic about the backup in customers had triggered an unprofessional and unnecessary outburst. Although he later apologized profusely to Greg, the damage was done. Greg worked his shift in a grim and stony silence, and everyone else avoided Jason for the entire evening.

Focus on the problem, not the person.

Greg was certainly wrong to be late, and it was Jason's duty to tell him so—but not in front of others. When we criticize someone in front of others, even if we do so in a calm manner, we will only make that person defensive. An employee who feels he or she has been criticized in an unfair manner will often not accept the point of the criticism, even if it is valid.

A good rule of thumb is to focus on the problem, not the person. A comment such as "You must think you're above the rules" is an attack on Greg, not on his lateness. By publicly attacking Greg, not Greg's performance, Jason broke the top two rules for offering criticism. His later apology could not undo the harm.

What should Jason have done? He should have waited until he was calmer and had all the facts. When we let emotion enter our criticism, it will have a negative effect—on the person we are criticizing and on our ability to be clear about the problem. We may end up making blanket statements, like Jason's "You do this all the time." It is important to be fair and exact about the facts of the situation. Exactly how often was Greg late? Were there any extenuating circumstances this particular time? Jason did not even give Greg a chance to explain why he was late.

Stick to one issue. Jason's mentioning Greg's inability to fill the salt and pepper shakers was poorly timed and inappropriate. This misstep shows that you should leave the evaluation of other tasks to a later discussion—focus on the issue at hand, instead.

Also, try to balance the criticism with some praise and some encouragement. It must be clear to you and the worker that there is a way to improve the situation. Ask if there is anything you can do to help. Be ready to offer some concrete suggestions.

It also helps to involve the worker in finding a solution to the problem. If lateness is truly part of a pattern, let the employee offer suggestions for solving his or her problem of getting to work on time.

Alexander Welsh, author of *The Skills of Management,* suggests asking questions that will involve the worker, such as, How do you feel about the situation? Is work going as well as you'd hoped? By encouraging the worker to participate in finding a solution, you may lessen his or her resentment.

Offering criticism is one of the most difficult jobs of any leader. Always keep in mind that the purpose of criticism is to help the other person become more effective. Keep the following things in mind when giving criticism:

- Balance the criticism with praise.

- Focus on the performance, not the person.

- State the problem privately, in a reasonable tone of voice.

- Be specific about the facts of the matter.

- Make sure you have all the facts.

- Discuss what has to be done to prevent the problem from happening again.

Offering criticism is one of the most difficult jobs of any leader.

By involving the other person in this process, you are more likely to get his or her cooperation to achieve the desired change. That, of course, is the ultimate goal of a good leader.

CONDUCTING PERFORMANCE REVIEWS

Say the phrase "performance review" to workers and they often respond: "boring!," "unproductive!," or "oh, no! Not more criticism of my job performance!" But well-planned performance reviews are worthwhile—for both managers and employees. As a leader, it is your responsibility to convey the value and importance of performance reviews to your employees. While performance reviews may be time consuming, they are an excellent chance to get to know your employees better (including listening to their feedback about the job) and establish clear cut goals and milestones for their development and advancement. Here are a few basic tips to make performance reviews more successful:

- *Learn the system.* Be sure that you understand your company's protocol for performance reviews ahead of the meeting. Some companies have elaborate systems in place; others ask their managers to largely wing it by creating their own review forms, etc.

- *Track your workers' progress.* Get in the habit of consistently recording your thoughts about your workers' accomplishments and strength/weaknesses during the year so that you have a paper trail that will help prepare you for the review.

- *Develop a plan for the review.* Be ready to laud your workers' accomplishments, provide constructive criticism, and tell each why or why not they will be receiving a raise and/or promotion. Establish goals and milestones for each employee to encourage professional growth.

- *Be a good listener.* Be sure to ask your employees for feedback on your comments and an honest assessment of their performance over the past year.

- *Follow up after the review.* Continue to track the progress of your workers and keep any promises (future meetings, raise, etc.) that you made during the review.

BE A MOTIVATOR

Leaders must have the cooperation of their followers. Leaders who use force or fear to manipulate others are not leaders—they are tyrants. Unfortunately, there are people in positions of leadership who do not know how to get others to cooperate.

LEADERSHIP RELIES ON SHARED GOALS

- Abraham Lincoln could not have pursued the Civil War if enough followers did not share his goals of preserving the Union and ending slavery.

- Martin Luther King, Jr. was certainly a compelling preacher, but his followers would not have endured beatings, jail, and even death if they had not believed so strongly in the goal of civil rights for all.

- Mahatma Gandhi's charisma was based on his inspirational example, but his followers also were motivated by their desire to free India from Britain's rule.

- Barack Obama is a gifted and inspirational leader, but he would not have won the 2008 presidential election if voters did not wholeheartedly share his belief in the necessity of change in American politics.

Management is nothing more than motivating other people.

—Lee Iacocca, U.S. automotive industry executive

President Barack Obama would not have been elected if voters did not share his belief in the necessity of change in American politics. (Charlie Neibergall, AP Photo)

The key to cooperation is motivation. There must be something of value for the follower. The greatest motivator is a shared goal. People who agree with a goal will join to accomplish it.

Often the role of a leader is to define a goal in terms that show its value to others. This may not be the same value the leader holds. For example, suppose a student wants to establish a soda-can recycling program at her school. Some students welcome the opportunity to do something positive for the environment—these students share her goal. Others can only be convinced

The key to cooperation is motivation.

✍️ EXERCISE

People are more apt to help if they understand and agree with a cause. Explain how you would convince someone to do one of the following:

- Recycle their newspapers
- Volunteer at a soup kitchen
- Sell candy bars to raise money for a scholarship fund
- Walk instead of drive to neighborhood errands
- Save old-growth forests in the Pacific Northwest

to participate when it is pointed out that all deposit money will be donated to the class trip fund.

GAINING THE SUPPORT OF YOUR FOLLOWERS

A leader may gain and keep the support of followers by listening to their ideas. This builds a good relationship between the leader and followers. The leader earns the followers' support by indicating his or her trust in the followers' abilities. The leader's willingness to hear the followers' opinions shows respect and a desire to understand their feelings. People respond to those who make the effort to understand them.

People deserve to be recognized for the good work that they do—a simple "thank you," particularly in public, will build loyalty. When praise is specific, it also becomes a good teaching tool. It points out well-done elements that could carry over to other tasks.

The way to get a worker's best effort is to point out what he does well. When you comment on a worker's strong points, he learns what is expected and is likely to repeat the good work. It is easy to forget to give positive feedback—when work is done well, we tend to take it for granted. But positive feedback is essential to keeping a worker on the right track.

—Ann Holt, hospital administrator

By offering positive feedback first, you create a more receptive atmosphere in which to mention any areas for improvement. Your followers will trust that you have their best interests at heart and that you will tell them what they need to know. They will look to you for guidance, realizing that you can help them achieve the success they desire.

SUPERVISING AND TRAINING OTHERS

Maggie Holahan works at a dry-cleaning store after school and on weekends. As an experienced worker, she often helps train new employees.

"Some things should come naturally, like a pleasant attitude with the customers," says Holahan.

"But I mention it anyway, and I try to set a good example. And I tell new people about the 'uniform' we wear—navy shirts and khaki pants. The owner is pretty relaxed about it, as long as the shirt has a collar and is tucked in. It bugs me when the older kids come in to work on their college breaks with their shirts hanging out."

"There's a lot to remember when you work the counter," Holahan continues. "The computer alone takes getting used to. It will make several different kinds of receipts, depending on whether the customer wants cleaning, laundering, or tailoring. Each process has its own menu of choices—pre-spotting, sizing, starch, box or hanger, crease or no crease, and so on. So while the new person watches me key the order in, I tell them in words what I am doing. Later, when I think they are ready, I'll have them do slips while I watch."

Most people want to feel good about themselves and what they do. A good supervisor helps others do their best by being clear about what to do and how to do it. Training a person takes time and effort. It shouldn't be left to chance or left up to the worker to figure out. It is the leader's responsibility to provide the direction his or her worker needs to do the job.

To waken interest and kindle enthusiasm is the sure way to teach easily and successfully.

—Tryon Edwards, American theologian

When training others, begin simply, giving an overall explanation of the job. Explain any unfamiliar terms and equipment. Then break the job down into individual procedures. In *The Skills of Management,* Alexander Welsh notes that it is invaluable to demonstrate procedures. He suggests this pattern for getting the best results:

1. Break up any instruction into steps of about one or two minutes of spoken instruction.

2. Pause at the end of each step to let the learner react or catch up.

3. Check the learner's understanding. Answer questions to clear up any confusion before going on. Demonstrate the step again if necessary.

4. When all steps have been explained and demonstrated, recap the whole procedure verbally.

5. Repeat the demonstration, one step at a time, explaining fully in detail each stage as you go.

6. Recap key stages verbally.

7. Have the learner try the procedure—talk him through it when necessary.

8. Point out errors as they occur in a noncritical manner.

9. Have the learner repeat the procedure if necessary.

POPULAR TRAINING METHODS

- Apprenticeships
- Famous speakers
- Formal education
- How-to manuals
- Internet guides
- Job shadowing
- Off-site conferences
- On-site workshops
- Seminars

Don't try to teach too many new procedures at once. Training should be an ongoing process. You probably didn't learn your job in a day. Make sure you show patience and a willingness to answer questions. Be realistic in your expectations.

HIGH EXPECTATIONS LEAD TO SUCCESS

Although it's important to be realistic about what others can accomplish, a leader can help by setting a good example and setting high standards. We've all known teachers who are sticklers about written work, for example. By forcing a student to rewrite an essay until it meets these high standards, the teacher has helped the student produce superior work.

In order to help a worker meet standards, you must monitor the worker's ongoing performance, particularly at first. Only then will you truly know how to help the worker improve. If mistakes are made, they can be noted and corrected as they happen. If you wait to see the end-product, you may not be able to pinpoint what went wrong, and the worker may not be able to correct the problem without starting over.

This does not mean that you have to look over a worker's shoulder constantly. Once you feel you have gotten the worker on the right track, you should give him or her more freedom. In *Frontiers of Leadership: An Essential Reader,* authors Michel Syrett and Clare Hogg advise trusting others to make decisions—even if this means having to live with some mistakes. People learn from their mistakes.

Syrett and Hogg further note that followers develop initiative when given a degree of freedom. They are willing to think for themselves, make and carry out decisions, and take on more responsibility. It is still your job to define a clear set of "core responsibilities" to be carried out. But leaving room for freedom of choice beyond those core responsibilities expresses your desire for the worker to take some initiative. It also shows your confidence in his or her abilities. People generally try to live up to our expectations.

Followers develop initiative when given a degree of freedom.

✍ EXERCISE

[Al]though I've always pushed myself hard . . . I [had] a volleyball coach in high school who expected a lot out of me. I was expected to be a leader at all times, on and off the court. In hindsight, I suppose it was good for me, in that it made me realize how difficult it can be to be a good leader; but at the time, I resented it. I was held to a different standard than others on the team, and that was hard to deal with.

Instead, he should have focused on pushing me hard on the court and during practice, rather than worrying about my academic or other extracurricular activities. I know he was doing it because he cared and wanted me to do well, but if I wasn't mature enough to know what I was doing, maybe it would be best for me to screw up and learn from the experience.

—*Shennan Harris, law school student*

Like Harris, did you ever have a teacher or coach who was a tough grader or who pushed you to work hard? Did his or her methods work in the long run?

LEADING OTHERS TO SUCCESS

No matter how competent you are, you will often need to work with and rely on others. If they understand and share your goal, they will be motivated to do a good job. In fact, as a leader, you are in a

Like all leaders, good coaches work to get the best effort out of each team member. (Clayton Stalter, Journal-Courier/The Image Works)

position to help others do their very best. Your good example and high expectations can encourage other people's best efforts. Your careful training can get them on the right track, and your praise and constructive criticism can help them improve. They will be willing to listen to you because you are willing to listen to them. By treating others fairly and telling them clearly and completely what you need them to do, you ensure the best possible results. You cannot truly succeed without the success of others.

✍ EXERCISE

In teaching someone how to do something new, we often take too much for granted. Even tasks that seem very simple to us may be confusing to someone else.

   On a piece of paper, outline the steps for performing a task you know how to do well. Then teach the task to someone who has never done it before. You may find that you need to go into much more detail than the steps you outlined on paper.

   Try teaching the task again, this time using the nine-step pattern for teaching a new procedure suggested by Alexander Welsh earlier in this chapter.

✔ TRUE OR FALSE: ANSWERS

Do You Know How to Work with Others?

1. All types of criticism are wrong.

False. Constructive criticism is an acceptable form of criticism in the workplace. It consists of polite and useful suggestions that aim to help your employees improve their job performance.

2. Fear is an excellent motivational tool for managers.

False. Never use fear to get your employees to do what you want. It is a sure-fire way to alienate them and get nothing done.

3. Training workers takes time and effort.

True. Few people master new job duties in one day. As a manager, you need to be cognizant that your employees will learn at different speeds. Be patient and willing to answer their questions during the training process.

4. As a manager, it's important to monitor a worker's performance during a project.

True. This is the only way to both ensure that the project is done well and that your employees learn from any mistakes or roadblocks they encounter during the project. But never micromanage your employees. Set attainable goals and periodically meet with your employees to ensure that they are being met.

IN SUMMARY . . .

- It pays to listen to others.
- Criticism, when constructive, can be beneficial.
- When giving criticism, be specific and be discreet.
- Balance criticism with positive feedback.

- When training others, be patient and break larger processes into steps.
- Leaders should know when to intervene and when to step back.

3

ORGANIZING A PROJECT

Jared is an analyst for the marketing-research division of Emco, an appliance manufacturer. His team's ongoing assignments often involve general research on the competition's product lines.

Recently the small appliance division of Emco needed immediate research on a new hair dryer just marketed by their rival, Binder Company. Emco was developing a new hair dryer of its own; if its features were too similar to Binder's, Emco would delay production until they could implement additions or modifications to their product.

The manager of development explained the situation to Jared and asked him to get his team on the problem right away. Jared welcomed the challenge—here was a way their work could make a direct contribution to the company. First he needed to jump-start his team.

"Listen up, people," he commanded his coworkers. "Our next project is Binder. Once again, they've

✔ TRUE OR FALSE?

Are You a Good Organizer?

1. Goals must be achievable.

2. Projects should be organized using the following steps: (1) State the goal and final deadline; (2) List all the tasks that must be done; and (3) Assign tasks to yourself and others.

3. A good leader is responsible for completing every task during a project.

4. Successful leaders are excellent judges of their employees' talents and abilities.

Test yourself as you read through this chapter. The answers appear on pages 86–87.

gotten to market ahead of us. I don't know how they do it, but it's our job to find out. We've got a chance to make Emco stronger in the marketplace. I know you guys will do a great job—you're the best. So I'm counting on you."

The team, with no specific knowledge of the hair dryer situation, assumed their assignment was another general examination of Binder's entire product line. Since they had ongoing research on Binder in the files, they decided among themselves that Nick, one member of the team, would update the files and prepare a report. The rest of the team resumed work on other things that seemed more important.

When Jared checked several days later on their progress, he was devastated to find out that only Nick was working on the Binder project. "Where's an assessment of Binder's new dryer? Why hasn't someone conducted a survey of households on the desired features in a handheld dryer?" Jared asked.

SURF THE WEB: WORKING IN TEAMS

EffectiveMeetings.com: Team Tips
   http://www.effectivemeetings.com/teams/
      teamwork/teamtips.asp

Manual for Working in Teams
   http://www.analytictech.com/mb021/teamhint.
      htm

Surviving the Group Project: A Note on Working in Teams
   http://web.cba.neu.edu/~ewertheim/teams/
      ovrvw2.htm#Introduction

Team Building
   http://www.meetingwizard.org/meetings/team-
      building.cfm

13 Ways to Encourage Teamwork
   http://www.askmen.com/money/
      successful_100/115_success.html

A leader has the responsibility to explain the purpose and goals of the work assigned to the team.

"What kind of dryer?" asked Nick. "Nobody said anything about doing dryer research in particular. How were we supposed to know?"

Jared failed in communicating the full scope of the project. In order to do a good job, people need to know what they should be trying to do and why they should be trying to do it. A leader has the responsibility to explain the purpose and goals of the work assigned to the team.

DEFINE TEAM GOALS

Goals must be clearly defined. Don't just say, "Take care of it" or "Get it done as soon as possible." In communicating a goal to a team, a leader must be as concrete as possible about what tasks must be done to reach the goal. It is important to be realistic about the amount of effort that will be needed for each task and to set a reasonable deadline for completing the project.

For example, the following statement by a manager of the employee-benefits division to his staff is not specific enough:

"Our goal is to inform employees about the choices for a new health plan."

A better goal would also state how and when this is to be accomplished:

"By September 12, all employees must be informed about the differences among the benefits and costs of the three proposed health plans. Our department will provide information sessions in Conference Room B from 11:00 A.M. to 12:00 P.M. every Thursday, from now until September 12."

The benefits staff can now readily see that they will need to prepare and present these information sessions to achieve their goal.

Goals must be specific, have a timetable, and be achievable. Goals that are too ambitious will discourage those who fear they cannot reach them. Goals that are too easy may breed carelessness or boredom. Good goals "stretch" workers and encourage them to put forth their best effort.

If goals are not clearly set, the result of a project is likely to be unsatisfactory. If people don't know exactly what they are supposed to do, chances are they won't do it or will do it incorrectly. A good leader shouldn't merely rely on a team to ask questions to determine their goals. If the team members receive too little or unclear information about a project, they may assume they missed something and make

✍ EXERCISE

Think of a time when you had to set a goal for yourself. Perhaps it was writing a resume, running your first 5K race, losing weight, learning a foreign language, or convincing someone to donate to a worthy cause. How did you set the goal up so you would achieve it? What difficulties did you have along the way? Did you set up a reward for achieving this goal?

incorrect guesses instead of asking for clarification. If people don't know why they are to do something, they may not care enough to do it well. This is human nature—if a leader doesn't care enough about the project to explain it properly, why should anyone care about doing it?

TEAM PARTICIPATION IN PROJECT DEVELOPMENT

Once a project's overall goal has been determined and communicated to the team, it is often possible to involve the members in decisions concerning the development of the project. This participation depends on the situation, the experience of the team, and the difficulty of the project. Participation has two benefits:

- Brainstorming sessions can yield many good ideas about how to proceed, who should do which assignments, and when individual tasks should be completed.

- The more you involve your team, the harder they are likely to work.

Effective motivators know that the involvement of those who will be part of the group trying to reach those goals is crucial to the outcome.

—J. W. McLean and William Weitzel in
Leadership—Magic, Myth, or Method

J. W. McLean and William Weitzel have surveyed
thousands of workers to ask specifically what motivates them the most. Strangely enough, money and
job security are not at the top of the list. The surveys
show that workers most value being appreciated, followed closely by "being an insider." Being an insider
may simply mean knowing the goals and purpose of
the work to be done or being informed about company developments. But workers included in some
of the decisions about goals and assignments may
feel most appreciated.

---

*The achievements of an organization are the results of
the combined effort of each individual.*

**—Vince Lombardi, legendary professional football
coach**

Workers want to feel a part of what they do. Corporate policies and management styles have changed
to allow more employee participation within all areas
of a business. Not only should workers feel included,
they should have pride in their accomplishments.
The most successful companies have employees who
are proud of what they do and whom they do it for.
These employees feel a direct connection with their
company's product or service. Successful companies
also allow open lines of communication between
employees and higher management. *Two-way communication*—information exchanged between a leader
and his or her team—should be the norm.

Hall of Fame football coach Vince Lombardi stressed that success could only be attained by the combined efforts of team members. (Bettmann/Corbis)

GET ORGANIZED

Although involving the team may have many rewards, it is ultimately the responsibility of the leader to organize the project. The project will not organize itself, and such a task cannot be left to chance.

"I really hated working on group projects in high school," says college freshman Alicia Barron. "Nobody was ever in charge. Nothing ever got done until the last minute, or two people ended up doing the same work, or parts of the project didn't get done at all. And you know that certain people always did most of the work, even though everybody got the same grade.

✏ EXERCISE

What motivates you to work hard? Make a photocopy of this page and circle all terms that apply.

Money	Learning more
Good grades	Good weather
Fame	Material goods
Success	Beauty
Challenges	Humor
Diversity	Religion
Food	Stability
Fun	Changes
Exercise	Security
Being liked	Appreciation

"I really like the system they have here, though," Barron continues. "In my honors seminar, I work with the same three other students on projects all semester long. We rotate the leader position with each new project. The leader decides how the work should be divided, who should do which parts, and when it should be completed. My partners are usually extremely fair."

Good order is the foundation of all good things.

—Edmund Burke, British philosopher

Being the leader may not be as simple as Barron describes it, especially if the project is complicated. It helps to organize your own thinking about the project. What are the individual tasks that need to be done in order to reach the project's goal? Who will do each task? When will each task need to be completed?

The more tasks involved in a project, the more organizational skills you need. Some tasks have to be performed one at a time, with each being finished before the next can be started. Sometimes several tasks can be handled at once. It depends on the nature of the project and the individual tasks.

The next step is to set a deadline for each task. Always schedule some extra time into the plan— problems are bound to come up. Finally, assign the tasks to yourself and others. Check that each person knows his or her assignments and the deadlines.

Organizing a project has five basic steps:

Always schedule some extra time into the plan—problems are bound to come up.

1. State the goal and final deadline.

2. List all the tasks that must be done.

3. Put those tasks in proper order.

4. Set a deadline for each task.

5. Assign tasks to yourself and others.

DELEGATE RESPONSIBILITY

The ultimate goal of a leader is to get the very best contribution from *all* members of the team—including the leader. At times, the leader will be the best person to do a particular task; if not, he or she should delegate the task to someone else.

Responsibility walks hand in hand with capacity and power.

—Josiah Gilbert Holland, American writer

Laura is the president of her church youth group. Part of the group's outreach program is providing holiday gifts for needy children. Every year the whole congregation helps out, but the youth group organizes the drive, wraps the gifts, and delivers them to the participating families.

✍ EXERCISE

Think of a time when you organized a project for school, an extracurricular club, or even at home. How did you break down the responsibilities? Did you follow any of the five steps for organizing a project? How did it work out in the end?

Each child's name, age, gender, and size have to be recorded on a master list and on an index card. The cards are then offered to any member of the congregation who wishes to buy a gift for a child. In years past, the index cards were written by hand, but Laura thought that the group should type the master list into Microsoft Excel. This way the information could be organized and printed as stick-on labels. Since Mark, the youth group's vice president, was knowledgeable about spreadsheet programs, Laura asked him if that was something he could do.

"Sure," said Mark. "I'm great with computers. I'll type the master list, produce the labels, and stick them on the index cards. No problem."

Laura told him generally what the cards needed to include, and Mark promised to have the cards ready in time for the congregation's service on Sunday.

When Mark brought the completed cards to the service, Laura was thrilled—that is, until she checked them. They had forgotten to include gender information on the cards, which posed a problem for children with ambiguous names such as Alex. Mark offered to add the gender information by hand, but there wasn't enough time. Many members of the congregation had planned to pick up a card during the coffee hour following the service.

"It's not your fault, Mark," Laura admitted. "I didn't think it through and tell you all you needed to know. I was just so thrilled to get someone to do it on the computer."

Laura was on the right track when she asked some-one else to do a task she was not comfortable doing. And perhaps Mark was the best person for that task. But Laura forgot to give him some important informa-tion. When delegating responsibility, be clear about what you need.

When to Delegate

A person in charge may delegate work to others for many reasons. Like Laura, there may be a task that someone other than the leader is more qualified to do. Or perhaps the leader realizes that he or she has so many responsibilities in overseeing the project that others will have to take on many of the tasks. Whatev-er the reason, it is unrealistic for the leader to assume all of the work on a project; likewise, it is unfair for the leader to delegate all of the work to the team. A good leader maintains a good balance between per-sonal involvement and team participation through delegation. A leader must also have realistic expecta-tions about what everyone can accomplish.

Ask yourself which of your activities could be done by somebody else—adequately, as well as you can, or even better than you can do it.

—Alexander N. Welsh, *The Skills of Management*

For many leaders, the problem with delegating is thinking that no one else can do the task as well. This

A leader must decide on the best use of his or her time.

may indeed be the case, but that should not necessarily stop a leader from delegating the task if somebody else can do an adequate job. A leader must decide on the best use of his or her time. Perhaps there are many other aspects of the project that only the leader can handle. In this case, he or she may need to delegate the less demanding tasks to others.

How to Delegate

Telling someone what to do requires a balanced approach. A hesitant tone can lead the other person to be unsure of your intention; an arrogant tone can lead to resentment. A feeling of mutual trust produces the best results. You trust someone on your team to do the task to the best of his or her ability. That person trusts you to provide the support needed to do it. This includes supplying all the information and materials needed and allowing adequate time to complete the task.

The key to delegation is the word **entrust.** *When you delegate, you entrust the entire matter to the other person, along with sufficient authority to make necessary decisions. This is quite a different thing from saying, "Just do what I tell you to do."*

—**Edwin C. Bliss in** *Getting Things Done: The ABC's of Time Management*

When delegating tasks to others, the leader needs to be as specific and detailed as possible. If possible, write down assignments for others. The clearer you are, the easier their job will be, and the better the results. The purpose in delegating is to save time and effort. The task may have to be redone if you're misunderstood.

ASSIGNING TASKS

Rebecca explains how her promotion to a leadership position within her marketing company has challenged her. "When I was first promoted, I was thrilled," says Rebecca. "Then reality set in. I used to just do what I was told. Now my boss comes to me with a project and a deadline and the rest is up to me. Well, not just me. I have a great team. But it's my job to make the best use of them. The hardest part is giving out assignments.

"At first, when I didn't know my team very well, I would list the tasks that needed to be done on a sheet of paper," Rebecca continues. "Then I'd have everybody indicate whether they were strong or weak in that kind of activity. The problem was that they were not always realistic. Usually they underestimated themselves. But I didn't know if they really thought a task was too hard or if they just didn't want too much work. Others overrated their strengths and I didn't know until it was too late that they were in over their heads.

"As I came to know their abilities better," continues Rebecca, "I felt more comfortable making assignments. But there are still problems. Some parts of a project are more involved than others and take more time. It takes a lot of experience to gauge the amount of effort a particular job will take. If I miscalculate, somebody is going to be overburdened and angry. I now keep a log of past assignments, including information on who did the job, how long it took, and how well it was done. It helps me to be more realistic about how long it takes to do certain types of jobs. It has also helped me build a profile of each member of the team. I note each person's strengths and weaknesses, styles of working, and assignment preferences.

As the manager of a small department charged with many responsibilities, one of my duties is to know the strengths of my staff and coworkers and delegate tasks accordingly. I rely on the fact that I can delegate certain projects to other workers and be assured that they will be satisfactorily completed. If I couldn't, there is no way I—or anyone else—would be able to single-handedly complete everything that the department is responsible for.

—Janet Canny, encyclopedia editor

"I can't always give them what they want," concludes Rebecca, "but I do avoid favoritism. An assignment should be based strictly on a person's ability to perform the job."

As Rebecca has found, one of the most difficult responsibilities a leader has is choosing the right

✍ EXERCISE

Make two lists: one listing your greatest strengths, the other listing some of your weaknesses. After considering these lists, what sort of tasks would you rather do yourself, and what tasks would you delegate to others? For example, if you are a math-minded person, perhaps you would like to balance a club's budget. Or if you are a good writer, perhaps you would like to take notes at a team meeting.

person for a particular task. A leader should never simply assign a complicated, multitask project to a team without sorting out who will do what. Sometimes the choice is obvious: A member of the team has demonstrated a clear and superior ability for a type of work. In other cases, the leader must consult with the team members to see if there are preferences for assignments. But the leader must still use his or her judgment to decide which worker is best suited to a particular task. Some people work best at assignments that are technical in nature. Others shine in situations that involve interacting with other people. Certain tasks require a great deal of patience; others require an immediate reaction. A leader must really know the job as well as his coworkers.

MAINTAINING OBJECTIVITY

It may be natural to give the best assignment, the easiest schedule, or the most credit to certain individuals. Perhaps they fully deserve your good attentions. But it is possible that you are being unfair to others who may also deserve a break. Avoid even the appearance of playing favorites. Vary assignments and schedules in a way that is fair to all. Avoid loading the least attractive tasks on the same person. If there are a number of those types of tasks throughout the project, a rotating schedule can be used from the start. Everyone can take a turn in doing the undesirable tasks.

Don't make judgments about people automatically or based on your feelings alone. Always question your objectivity. Do the facts back up your opinion? Is a highly likable, outgoing worker really the best person for this particular task? Perhaps, but you may be overlooking a quiet but more competent worker. You also need to be aware of your own blind spots and prejudices. People are individuals and deserve to be treated as such.

Also, everyone deserves a second chance. Perhaps there is someone who once did a poor job for you. Be sure you view this worker's current capabilities objectively. There may have been circumstances that interfered with his or her earlier performance. It's important that you have a realistic understanding of the pressures and needs of others. As a leader, you should know all about the members of your team—their strengths as well as their weaknesses—so that you can lead them effectively.

CHARTING YOUR COURSE

When a project requires the completion of a number of tasks, a chart can help the team visualize the course they will need to follow. Here are a few examples of charts that will help you complete projects.

Flow Charts

A *flow chart* shows each task in sequence. In order to make a flow chart, first make a list of tasks that will have to be done to reach your project's goal. Then put the tasks in the order in which they must be done. Use boxes to show tasks and diamonds to indicate decision points. These diamond checkpoints can keep you from going ahead when you may actually need to go back to a previous task. See the following sample flow chart for planning a reception for an honored guest.

The diamonds show points where things might get held up: invitees who have not confirmed their attendance and the approval of your news release. In the first case, if all confirmations are not in, you cannot yet order the food. In the second case, your superior may ask you to redraft the news release before you send it to the newspapers. The side arrows send you back to the step that will need to be redone.

Although a basic flow chart does not indicate who will do each task or when it is due, you can add this

SAMPLE FLOW CHART

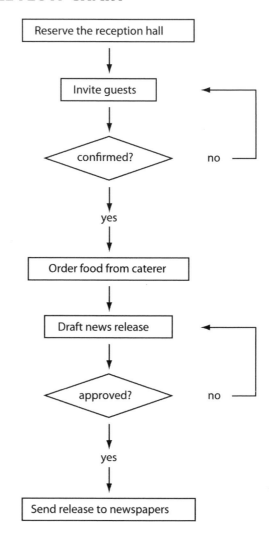

SURF THE WEB: FLOW CHARTS

Flowcharting Help Page
http://home.att.net/~dexter.a.hansen/flowchart/
flowchart.htm

Gliffy: Flow Charts
http://www.gliffy.com/free-flow-chart-software

Inc.com: Flow Charts
http://www.inc.com/encyclopedia/flow-charts.html

Mind Tools: Flow Charts
http://www.mindtools.com/pages/article/
newTMC_97.htm

information to each box. The flow chart can be a very useful tool in organizing a project.

Gantt Charts

A flow chart shows tasks to be done in sequence. Sometimes tasks go on simultaneously. A simple horizontal chart, called a *Gantt chart,* can show the timing of both sequential and simultaneous tasks. Since this type of chart shows the relative amount of time allocated to each task, it is also called a *time/ task analysis chart.*

The first column down the left side of the chart lists the tasks in the order that they will be performed.

✍ EXERCISE

Create a Gantt chart for a team of three to prepare and present an oral report. Use lined paper to show the timing of five or more tasks for this project.

All tasks, including relatively simple ones, should be listed.

The next column is filled in with the name of the person assigned to the task. A person may be assigned more than one task. These assignments may

SURF THE WEB: GANTT CHARTS

Brief Tutorial on Gantt Charts
http://www.me.umn.edu/courses/
me4054/assignments/gantt.html

Gantt Chart
http://www.ganttchart.com

What is a Gantt Chart?
http://www.brighthub.com/office/
project-management/articles/
6550.aspx

SAMPLE GANTT CHART

Task	Assigned	2/11	2/12	2/13	2/14	2/15	2/18	2/19	2/20	2/21	2/22
Reserve room	Ellen	■									
Send memos	Max	■									
Develop activities	Jane	■	■								
Prepare activity sheets	Jane/Max		■	■	■	■					
Reserve equipment	Ellen			■	■						
Print materials	Ellen						■	■	■		
Collate folders	Ellen									■	
Conduct workshop	Jane/Max										■

be provisional at first. As you analyze how much time is required for each task, you may need to shift assignments.

The top row of the chart is a time line from the project's start date to its end date. The time line can be expressed in days, weeks, or months—whichever is appropriate. The shaded area connects the start and end dates of an individual task.

Take a look at the sample Gantt chart for planning a workshop. By looking at the shaded areas, you can tell which tasks will go on simultaneously. Some related activities even overlap. For example, preparing activity sheets can begin while some workshop activities are still being developed. The chart also shows that equipment should not be reserved until all activities have been planned.

✔ TRUE OR FALSE: ANSWERS

Are You a Good Organizer?

1. Goals must be achievable.

True. Never set goals that can't be met. They create overworked and disillusioned employees.

2. Projects should be organized using the following three steps: (1) State the goal and final deadline; (2) List all tasks that must be done; and (3) Assign tasks to yourself and others.

False. There are actually five steps: (1) State the goal and final deadline; (2) List all the tasks that must be done; (3) Put those tasks in proper order; (4) Set a deadline for each task; and (5) Assign tasks to yourself and others. If you forget to rank the tasks in order of importance, you might end up spending too much time on less important duties. If you fail to assign deadlines for each task, you might delay the completion of the entire project.

3. A good leader is responsible for completing every task during a project.

False. No leader, whether it's Barack Obama, Carly Fiorina, or Steve Jobs, can do it all. Successful leaders delegate responsibility to their employees.

4. Successful leaders are excellent judges of their employees' talents and abilities.

True. Good managers are keenly aware of their employees' strengths and weaknesses and assign tasks accordingly. They also avoid playing favorites and refrain from making judgments about their employees based on their own personal biases.

IN SUMMARY . . .

- Leaders must be able to explain the needs of a project, including what exactly needs to be done and why it is important.

- Goals and standards must be set high enough to motivate people to work hard, but not so high that they are impossible to achieve.

- Different things can motivate people. Good leaders should find out what motivates their team to encourage hard work and give their team a sense of fulfillment.

- Organizing a project is crucial to getting work done well and on time. This organization can take different forms, and should be determined on the basis and scope of the project.

- Leaders cannot and should not try to do everything themselves. Tasks need to be delegated to other members of the team, according to their interests, talents, and abilities.

- Use tools such as flow charts and Gantt charts to stay organized and on track.

4

COMPLETING
A PROJECT

Planning the sales conference is a big responsibility, but I am confident that you'll do a good
job," Mr. Kane told Tom, one of his strongest managers. "You've got a great team, and I'll assist you
in any way I can. Now let's sit down and discuss
the focus of our next conference. I'll leave planning
the actual agenda to you and your team," Mr. Kane
said.

But when Tom returned to his department, he
began to worry. There were so many things to do to
plan the sales conference. He called his team together
to tell them the news.

"Our goal is to plan a three-day sales conference
to be held June 12 through the 14th in Omaha,
Nebraska. The agenda will focus on developing an
international market," Tom explained.

The team immediately started brainstorming,
generating a long list of tasks that would need to be
accomplished over the coming months. Eventually,

✔ TRUE OR FALSE?

Do You Know How to Complete a Project?

1. It is better to turn in quality work late than submit average or poor work on time.

2. Using a wall calendar is an excellent way to monitor a small project.

3. Managers should constantly look over their employees' shoulders to ensure projects are on schedule.

4. Throughout a project, leaders should provide both constructive criticism and positive reinforcement to workers.

Test yourself as you read through this chapter. The answers appear on pages 105–106.

Tom scheduled a meeting for the following week and sent them back to their regular duties.

Over the next several days, Tom worked on creating an assignment chart to present at the next meeting. It wasn't too difficult deciding who would do what. His team had planned a half-day workshop two months ago. He had been impressed with the team's cooperation and had come to know each member's capabilities. The short workshop had gone extremely well.

"The difference is that this time it's three days," he thought. "We have to take into account transportation, hotel arrangements, outside speakers, catering, and recreation. I'm sure we're forgetting some things. I'd better get the team started on all of this right away. That way, when something else pops up, we'll have time to deal with it," Tom thought to himself.

At the meeting the following week, Tom unveiled a Gantt chart that organized all the tasks that needed to be done for the conference to run smoothly. The column of tasks seemed to go on forever. "We're going to be really busy around here," Tom admitted. "Let me know if any of you have any conflicts."

His team diligently began making notes in daybooks and pocket calendars. "I have a problem," said Paul. "If I do all my assignments for this project that are due in the next two weeks, I won't be able to get any of my regular work done."

"This is hard to follow," said Hilary. "I keep losing my place on the chart. My name is all over the place. I'm afraid I'm going to miss one of my assignments."

Ed agreed. "I'm not sure I can understand the chart, either. I think this may be too big a project to have plotted out in just one chart. I'd suggest that we reorganize the tasks. Put all the planning tasks in one group, including planning the agenda, choosing the speakers, and researching recreational opportunities. Then group the logistical tasks, such as sending out notices, making travel and hotel arrangements, and booking the speakers."

"Great idea, Ed," said Tom. "You and I are responsible for the planning tasks, so I'll make a chart for us. But the logistical tasks will have to be broken down even further. I'll work on a new kind of chart that will help each person see his or her duties more easily. And I'll reconsider the due dates for some of the assignments. Thank you all for your honesty, and Ed, for your idea."

Tom was fortunate that his team spoke up. If they hadn't voiced their concerns, Tom would have assumed everything was okay. But due dates must be realistic to take into account other work that must be done and to allow for delays, problems, and corrections. In addition, a chart that is too complicated to follow is no help at all.

As the leader, Tom needs to provide the team with a clear way to follow their tasks through the project. For example, Hilary's basic responsibility, to secure the hotel, involved three separate tasks that were, as Hilary pointed out, "all over" the Gantt chart. Selecting a hotel was one of the first things that needed to be done, but booking it would not come until later. Final confirmation on the number of rooms would be months away. As a result, Hilary's tasks were well separated on the Gantt chart and very confusing to follow.

TASKS-BY-LEVELS CHARTING

Tom wants to create a chart that will list closely related tasks together. The tasks are presented in a

SAMPLE TASKS-BY-LEVELS CHART

Level 1			Level 2			Level 3		
Due	**To**	**Task**	**Due**	**To**	**Task**	**Due**	**To**	**Task**
10/7	HJ	Gather hotel brochures	11/25	HJ	Book hotel	3/30	HJ	Confirm hotel
10/9	DL	Estimate # of attendees	12/15	DL	Send notices to attendees	4/3	DL	Select menus
10/11	FB	Contact travel agent for information	4/1	FB	Make travel arrangements	4/9	FB	Reserve golf course
11/30	PG	Book speakers	4/1	PG	Order audio-visual equipment	6/11	PG	Supervise equipment installation

group so that each team member can easily identify his or her specific responsibilities. The kind of chart Tom should use is called a *tasks-by-levels chart*. This type of chart was designed by Stephanie Winston, author of *The Organized Executive: The Classic Program for Productivity: New Ways to Manage Time, Paper, People and the Digital Office*. In this chart, tasks are divided by levels and put into columns.

Take a look at Tom's new tasks-by-levels chart. Hilary's tasks appear in separate columns, but she can see them all together by reading across the top line of the chart.

Note the following:

- *Level 1 tasks* go in the first column. These tasks can be carried out first because they do not depend on other tasks. For example, Hilary can gather hotel brochures.

- *Level 2 tasks* depend on the completion of one or more Level 1 tasks. In this example, once research has been done, Hilary can book the hotel that has the facilities her company needs. This task would be listed in the second column.

- *Level 3 tasks* cannot be done until the completion of one or more Level 2 tasks. In this instance, Hilary would wait to make a final confirmation until she had a list of attendees. This task would be listed in the last column.

The tasks-by-levels chart makes it easier for workers to see their various assignments. It also helps them to see the relationships and dependencies between tasks and the order in which tasks must be done. When a project is long term and complicated, grouping tasks in this way can help everyone keep track of assignments.

MONITOR TEAM PROGRESS

Sarah is the editor-in-chief of the Lincoln High School yearbook. She is bright, dedicated, and has a talented staff. The only problem seems to be deadlines.

✍ EXERCISE

Your school is planning a carnival to benefit the local children's hospital. Organize the following list of tasks into three levels. You will have three tasks in each level. Remember that you must complete Level 1 tasks before Level 2 tasks, and Level 2 tasks must be done before those in Level 3.

- Set up game booths
- Get permit for a town playground
- Prepare food
- Advertise in newspaper and on radio
- Order food supplies
- Plan games
- Rent amusement rides
- Rent food tent
- Purchase prizes

"I've worked on the past three yearbooks," says Sarah, "and we never missed a single deadline before. This year we've really had a lot of problems. I try to keep after everybody, but there's so much to keep track of. Sometimes it isn't our fault. For example, a

Leaders cannot rely on memory alone. They need to develop a system to monitor progress.

computer virus destroyed eight pages of the senior section. But many of our problems are caused by members of the staff simply not doing their jobs on time.

"Even so," continues Sarah, "I always feel like it's my fault. I wish I could figure out a way to monitor each and every task. Because of all the late fees we had to pay for those missed deadlines, we went over our budget. We had planned to use spot color for headlines in every section. Now we can only afford it in the Senior Life section. We're all so disappointed."

Sarah's disappointment is understandable. She has devoted a lot of time to planning and producing the yearbook. Because of late fees, it won't have the look she had envisioned.

In business, missing a deadline can be very costly and have serious consequences. The leader must find a way to keep track of the various tasks that need to be done and when they need to be completed. Leaders cannot rely on memory alone. They need to develop a system to monitor progress. There are many ways to do this; leaders need to choose the system that best fits their situation.

Notebook Tracking

If a project is relatively simple, you can use a method called *notebook tracking* to monitor the progress. Decide on the order in which the jobs need to be done. Assign each task a page in your notebook in sequence. Record the details that apply to the task, such as who has been assigned the task, the deadline for that task, and the date you intend to check on its progress. Deadlines and dates for progress checks should also be recorded on your calendar. Here is how a notebook page might look:

Task: Order food
To: Margaret
Due: February 16
Progress check: February 9
I have entered these dates in my calendar.
I have made the progress check.
Task is completed.

Calendars

No matter what system you choose to monitor your team's progress, you will always need to rely on a calendar to prompt you. For example, flow charts, Gantt charts, or tasks-by-levels charts all need to be backed up by recording due dates on a calendar. If you made a task/assignment chart in a project's planning stage, post it where all team members can see it. This will help them follow the sequence of tasks. But the chart alone will not help you, as leader, check their progress and monitor deadlines. You will need to develop a checking system.

Often a large wall calendar or month-at-a-glance poster will be sufficient for monitoring a simple project. Enter each task and the name of the assigned person on the task's due date. Use a different colored marker for each person. As each task is completed, cross it off with a bold black diagonal line. This will make it evident what tasks have not been completed. The unmarked squares are your prompts to check on the status of those tasks.

If there are many tasks in a project, you will need to set actual dates for progress checks; record these dates on your own desk calendar. These progress checks

✍ EXERCISE

Make two more notebook pages patterned on the preceding one. Use any two tasks from Tom's sales conference tasks-by-levels chart depicted earlier in this chapter. Remember to set a progress-check date that provides enough time to solve problems and make any necessary corrections.

should be well enough in advance of the actual due dates to allow time for correcting any problems. If corrections need to be made, enter a "recheck" date on your desk calendar.

It is important, however, to avoid "overmanaging" the project. If you are always looking over your workers' shoulders, they may not do anything without reminders or help from you. Progress checks are simply for your overall control and to reinforce *worker* accountability.

Team Meetings

A leader may choose to monitor a project and check on progress toward deadlines by scheduling regular team meetings. During meetings, members can report on the status of their assigned tasks. Everyone has the opportunity to see where everyone else is on the project. The leader can check on the team's progress and help workers deal with any problems. Priorities are set and adjustments may be made to the schedule.

The ability to work with coworkers with varying personality types, work skills, and even egos is essential to your success as a project manager (PM). The success of a project often is dependent on the combined efforts of a team, but these efforts must be led and directed by a dedicated and flexible PM.

—Nora Kerr, information technology project manager, Omicron Technologies

An added benefit of meetings is that they can clear up any misconceptions about the project. Someone's question may help the whole team come to a better understanding of an issue. Meetings also provide the opportunity for a leader to probe the team's feelings about the project. Perhaps they are feeling

SURF THE WEB: IMPROVE YOUR MEETINGS

EffectiveMeetings.com
  http://www.effectivemeetings.com

Meeting Wizard
  http://www.meetingwizard.com

Mind Tools: Running Effective Meetings
  http://www.mindtools.com/CommSkll/
    RunningMeetings.htm

Work911.com: Effective Meetings
  http://www.work911.com/articles/meetmgt.htm

overwhelmed by the workload. It may be time for the leader to add staff, even if just temporarily. For example, a manger may borrow workers from other related departments during busy periods.

☞ FACT

Interaction between leaders and subordinates results in greater group output. Several studies have shown that managers who receive subordinate feedback are more effective on the job than managers who do not solicit such feedback.

Meetings allow for two-way feedback between the leader and his or her subordinates. Issues may be brought up during a meeting that the leader could not have discovered by simply monitoring deadlines. The disadvantage of meetings is that they take time. Many leaders, therefore, use meetings only infrequently and in combination with one of the other methods for checking progress described earlier in this chapter.

Meetings allow for two-way feedback between the leader and his or her subordinates.

EVALUATE PROGRESS

As a leader follows the progress of the team toward the project's goal, there will be times when he or she may have to point out faults and suggest corrections. But the leader's attitude should be one of guidance and support, not scolding or punishment. The leader's purpose is to evaluate the team's efforts and make adjustments as necessary. The objective is to move the team toward the project's goal.

People need to know how they are getting along and what progress they are making . . . . Often, the most effective way to speed up what is being done is to give recognition and commendation to those who deserve it, and thus spur them to greater effort.

—Ray A. Killian in Leadership on the Job

"I don't think I could ever go through that again," Adam admitted, after getting back from his company's annual event called Work Weekend. "It certainly was a worthwhile goal, but the process of getting there was a killer."

Every fall the entire company put aside a weekend to repair the houses of senior citizens. Adam was glad he worked for a company with a social conscience, but this year the job of coordinating the project had fallen to his department. They had nearly gone crazy organizing the weekend, and many things had gone wrong.

"There has to be a better way," he thought. "It's a good thing we're having a team meeting tomorrow." Carrie, his department head, had called the meeting to assess the department's handling of Work Weekend.

"The first thing I'd like to say is thank you all so much," Carrie began. "We weatherized and repaired over 30 homes. But we did have a lot of problems that I'd like to talk about. Even though another department will rotate into the coordinator's position next year, I still feel we can offer them the benefit of our experience. And believe it or not, the troubles we had with Work Weekend may carry over into other areas in our department. So let's see where things went wrong."

Carrie had come to the meeting armed with the original flow chart she had developed many weeks ago. Looking at the chart immediately triggered Adam's memory.

✍ EXERCISE

Meetings often get a bad reputation for being a waste of time for those involved because of unrelated chatting, lengthy lectures, or simply having no focus. Think of a time when this has happened to you. Who was responsible for the meeting and who was responsible for getting the meeting off track? Now think of a time when you participated in a productive meeting. What was done differently?

"I was in charge of purchasing supplies," he said, "but I had to have Mr. Cole sign every purchase order [P.O.]. Tracking him down wasn't always easy. If I left the P.O. on his desk, he might not get it back to me for several days. Maybe he could designate a second person to act on these special requests—someone who's more available."

Carrie told Adam she thought that was a good idea and promised to forward his suggestion to Mr. Cole. The team continued to study the steps of the flow chart to see where there had been lapses or bottlenecks. Another problem was wasting time making multiple trips to the hardware store. After some brainstorming, the team developed a solution: Next year, the company would send out a detailed questionnaire to the homeowners. This way, the

✍ EXERCISE

Almost everyone has worked at some time or another on a project that, while good intentioned, did not turn out as planned and organized. Maybe it was a school car wash or a field trip that you and other students helped to organize or a group presentation for class. Evaluate one of these projects and identify what went right and what could have been done better. Could the use of organizational tools such as flow charts, Gantt charts, or tasks-by-levels charts have helped you? Did the project suffer because of poor communication and infrequent team meetings? Write a short analysis of the project with suggestions for future students about how to better organize it.

workers would have more information about the needs of each homeowner and could order most of the supplies in advance.

By the time the meeting was over, the team felt satisfied that they had done a good job of assessing their project and suggesting improvements for the future. They also felt that Carrie appreciated their efforts, however imperfect. More important, she had demonstrated her respect for their opinions.

Not all project assessments involve a meeting. Sometimes the team leader prepares a written report for his or her manager. In this case, the leader will often consult with the team in drafting the report. He or she may ask the team members to respond to a questionnaire about their experience with the project.

When a project is completed, there is a tendency to breathe a sigh of relief, no matter what the outcome. But in order for a team to improve, it must look at the project objectively. Many small, seemingly minor glitches in a project may add up to a less-than-satisfactory result. In addition, problems that are not corrected are bound to occur in another project.

✔ TRUE OR FALSE: ANSWERS

Do You Know How to Complete a Project?

1. It is better to turn in quality work late than submit average or poor work on time.

False. It's extremely important to develop a reputation for turning in work on time. If you need extra time to complete a project, ask for it ahead of time.

2. Using a wall calendar is an excellent way to monitor a small project.

True. Tracking small projects with the help of a calendar is an effective way to ensure that every step of a project is accomplished.

3. Managers should constantly look over their employees' shoulders to ensure projects are on schedule.

False. Effective leaders periodically meet with their employees to assess project goals and deadlines. They do not micromanage their employees—which can often lead to workplace stress and reduced productivity.

4. Throughout a project, leaders should provide both constructive criticism and positive reinforcement to workers.

True. Providing constructive criticism is fine, but be sure to also recognize your employees' positive contributions.

IN SUMMARY . . .

- Before starting a project, group tasks into levels based on when they need to be done.

- Leaders should use tools such as notebook tracking, tasks-by-levels charts, calendars, and meetings to monitor a team's progress.

- Meetings, when conducted correctly, can be productive and allow two-way feedback between the leader and the team members.

- After a project is completed, assess how well it was organized and if anything could be done differently to have made the process run more smoothly.

5

LEARNING TO LEAD

"This is making me crazy," thought Dan as he sat staring out of his office window. "I've won the Art Director's Club design award twice, and this company won't even give me a chance at the assistant art director's position. I can't for the life of me figure out what's wrong."

Dan had majored in graphic design at a prestigious art college on the East Coast. When he graduated, he was thrilled to land a job as a graphic designer for a book publisher. Designing book covers combined his love of art with his love of reading and computer technology. His education had prepared him for graphic design, a skill in strong demand in the publishing industry. Everyone had thought Dan was on the fast track to success, especially Dan himself.

But when the assistant art director's position became vacant, Dan was passed over for the promotion. One of the other designers, a new employee named Kristen, commiserated with him over his

✔ TRUE OR FALSE?

Are You Ready to Lead?

1. Personal appearance matters in the workplace—especially for managers.

2. I can wear anything I want on Casual Friday.

3. Successful leaders don't just issue orders: They lead by example.

4. Mentors are more experienced coworkers who offer to show you the ropes on the job.

Test yourself as you read through this chapter. The answers appear on pages 136–137.

disappointment. "You're very talented. I think they're going to be sorry they didn't move you up," she said. "Do you even have a clue why they passed you by?"

"Mike thinks it's the way I look, but that seems shallow," Dan reasoned. "I mean, who cares these days? I've always worn jeans and Birkenstocks and I always will. It shouldn't matter how I dress, as long as I can do the work."

But when Dan finally worked up his courage to approach Jack, the art director, he was shocked to find out that his appearance had indeed been a major factor in the company's decision not to advance Dan. "It's not just talent, Dan," said Jack. "The assistant art director is a leadership position. The company was worried you were too young anyway, and your appearance just confirmed that opinion. I'm sorry."

"This is so unbelievably unfair," sputtered Dan. "And why didn't somebody say anything?"

"I did," said Jack. "Maybe I was too casual about how I said it, but don't you remember my comment the day you wore that tie-dyed shirt to the editors' meeting? And the time you colored your hair yellow? Your response both times was just a smile. I figured you were happy to be a designer and had no plans to move up. That's the message you were sending with your appearance. And I don't think we were reading you wrong. If you had really wanted to be in a leadership position, you would have made an effort to look the part."

DRESS FOR SUCCESS

Whether we like it or not, appearance does matter. People will generally have more confidence in someone who is professionally dressed and well groomed. Dressing professionally does not necessarily mean wearing a dress or suit and tie. It depends on the position, the organization, and even in which part of the country the organization is located.

Certain creative fields, such as music, art, and advertising, are thought to be more accepting of individual expression in clothing style. In his book *Jobsmarts for Twentysomethings*, Bradley G. Richardson offers this advice: "Just remember, it's the work that shows how creative you are, not how you dress."

READ MORE ABOUT IT: DRESSING FOR SUCCESS

Henderson, Veronique, and Pat Henshaw. *Image Matters for Men: How to Dress for Success!* London, U.K.: Hamlyn, 2007.

Lenius, Oscar. *A Well-Dressed Gentleman's Pocket Guide.* London, U.K.: Prion, 2006.

Lerner, Dick. *Dress Like the Big Fish: How to Achieve the Image You Want and the Success You Deserve.* Omaha, Neb.: Bel Air Fashions Press, 2008.

Peres, Daniel. *Details Men's Style Manual: The Ultimate Guide for Making Your Clothes Work for You.* New York: Gotham, 2007.

Weingarten, Rachel C. *Career and Corporate Cool.* Hoboken, N.J.: Wiley, 2007.

Dress-for-success books recommend dressing as well or better than the industry standard if you want respect. Even if a workplace is casual, someone who aspires to a leadership position will make sure he or she dresses appropriately. In some places this may simply mean dressing in a collared shirt tucked into neat jeans. In more conservative workplaces, this may mean a button-down shirt and khakis. Take your

cue from workers who are in the level you hope to
achieve. Also, if your company has "dress-down Fri-
days," don't overdo the casual look if you are serious
about a leadership position.

You may feel that it shouldn't matter how you dress.
You are the same person under whatever clothes you
wear. This is true, but like it or not, your appearance
can inspire confidence—and inspiring confidence is
your job if you want to lead.

Your appearance can inspire confidence— and inspiring confidence is your job if you want to lead.

BODY ADORNMENTS AND OTHER CONSIDERATIONS

People have preconceived ideas about how leaders
should look. In the workplace, this does not usually

WHAT IS "BUSINESS CASUAL?"

Corporate executives decide on dress
policies depending on the company's work
environment, culture, and business activity.
Business casual can be as lax as jeans,
sneakers, and T-shirts, or as conservative as
khaki pants, collared shirts, and loafers. It is
important for new workers to observe the
attire of their coworkers and superiors and
dress accordingly.

include sporting attention-getting body adornments. Indulge in obvious tattoos at your own peril. Facial piercing should be limited to the ears, and limit the number or earrings in general. Again, note what is acceptable by observing people in positions to which you aspire. Very large, flashy jewelry on any part of the body is viewed as unprofessional in many fields. Understated accessories are best.

Your perfume or cologne should also be understated. You want people to notice your accomplishments,

SURF THE WEB: WHAT TO WEAR-BUSINESS CASUAL

About.com: Business Casual Dress Code
   http://humanresources.about.com/od/
   glossaryd/g/dress_code.htm

Business Casual Attire
   http://www.career.vt.edu/JOBSEARC/BusCasual.
   htm

How to Dress Business Casual—Men
   http://www.ehow.com/how_41_dress-business-
   casual.html

How to Dress Business Casual—Women
   http://www.ehow.com/how_49_dress-business-
   casual.html

not your fragrances. Good grooming may of course include the use of scents—just be restrained. It is far more important to have clean clothes, hair, and fingernails. Make the effort. Show that you care about your appearance.

If you still question the importance of appearance in attaining a leadership position, consider this: A willingness to present a leaderlike appearance demonstrates maturity, which is an undeniable characteristic of a leader.

LEADING BY EXAMPLE

If you want to be a leader, you can't just "talk the talk," you need to "walk the walk." Leadership is all about following up your words with actions. In order to gain the respect of your staff and other employees, you need to always follow the rules of the company and have the highest ethics. This ranges from the little issues like arriving to work on time and following the company dress code to major issues such as never lying to your boss or fudging expense reports. Your employees are watching every move you make, and if you set a bad example, how can you expect them to do the right thing?

BODY LANGUAGE

"Kelly, take this file to Mr. Eckhart's office," requested her manager. "Be sure you deliver it to him personally. He likes to meet new staffers."

When Kelly had started work the previous week, Mr. Eckhart, the head of her division, had been away on a business trip. Now Kelly waited nervously in his reception area. Meeting new people had always been hard for Kelly, especially when the person was a superior. "Thank goodness I'm wearing this blazer," Kelly thought." At least I look like I belong here. But I sure don't feel like I do." She slumped further down in her seat and stared at the file she was holding.

When Mr. Eckhart came to his doorway, Kelly pushed herself out of her low chair. As he extended his hand, Kelly began to give him the file—until she realized he was offering to shake hands. Embarrassed, she looked down at her shoes and put her hand limply in his. "It's very nice to meet you," she nearly whispered. Then, handing him the file, she continued to stare at it as he welcomed her to the company. After he wished her a good day, she thanked him and fled the reception area. Mr. Eckhart just shook his head and returned to his office.

Kelly's body language gave a very negative impression to Mr. Eckhart. With conscious effort, you can learn to inspire confidence through positive body language. Stand and sit up straight. Act as if you deserve to be noticed. At the same time, be sure to notice others. Don't look down or away from someone—look the other person right in the eye. Eye contact inspires trust; a lack of eye contact makes you look suspicious. Just shy, you say? Leaders are not shy, so practice if you must. If you pretend to be comfortable, eventually you will be. And when you are comfortable, it puts others at ease.

Act as if you deserve to be noticed. At the same time, be sure to notice others.

Always offer your hand to someone . . . . A handshake is a friendship gesture and a professional courtesy. It's an open, welcoming gesture that makes people feel more comfortable around you.

—**Bradley G. Richardson** in *Jobsmarts for Twentysomethings*

Handshakes are an example of body language that speaks volumes. Richardson suggests that you grasp a person's hand firmly, give a squeeze, and hold until

A simple handshake may seem like a minor gesture, but when done correctly, it exudes confidence and politeness and can make a strong impression on others. (Artiga Photo/Corbis)

the other person breaks away or releases pressure. And of course, look the person right in the eye while you're doing it. Making eye contact when greeting someone expresses congeniality and self-confidence, both of which are looked upon favorably in the business world.

When we look someone in the eye, we also indicate that we are paying attention. Maintaining that eye contact shows that we are interested in what a person has to say. Leaning slightly toward a person has the same effect. Active listening is a characteristic of all good leaders.

THE IMPORTANCE OF BODY LANGUAGE

When interviewing or trying to impress superiors, watch what you are doing as well as what you are saying. Fidgeting can impart a sense of nervousness. Mindlessly playing with your hair can give someone the sense that you are easily distracted. Scratching can lend to thoughts of uncleanliness. Crossing your arms in front of you (instead of leaving them by your sides) can represent closemindedness or a cold personality. It may seem shallow or unfair, but these small and common mistakes can cost you a job or a promotion someday!

SURF THE WEB: BODY LANGUAGE

Answers.com: Body Language
   http://www.answers.com/topic/body-language

Gestures: Body Language and Nonverbal
Communication
   http://www.csupomona.edu/~tassi/gestures.
      htm#gestures

What the Boss' Body Language Says
   http://hotjobs.yahoo.com/career-articles-what_
      the_boss_body_language_says-306

Reassessing Body Language and Cultural Norms in a Global Workforce

As the U.S. workforce becomes more diverse and a growing number of companies do business abroad, it is important to keep in mind that body language and cultural traditions vary greatly throughout the world. For example, Americans often consider those who do not make eye contact as aloof, unconfident, or having something to hide. But this isn't true in all cultures. Some Asian cultures actually consider excessive eye contact to be rude. Other countries may restrict physical contact (such as handshakes) between men and women in business settings. If you interact with workers from other cultures it is a good idea to study their culture to learn what is socially acceptable and unacceptable. Some excellent resources that will help you learn more about cultural norms outside the U.S. include *Culture-Grams* (Proquest LLC, 2008) and *Multicultural Manners: Essential Rules of Etiquette for the 21st Century* (Wiley, 2005).

SPEAK LIKE A LEADER

Leaders must also be able to communicate their ideas to others. Becoming an effective speaker takes effort, practice, and sometimes even professional training. But even if you do not foresee giving speeches in public, it's important to be aware of how you speak. People judge us by the way we talk, as well as by what we say. For better or worse, our manner of speaking creates an instant impression on others.

Many speech "problems" are really just bad habits. Adding words such as "um," "like," and "you know" is common. Ask a friend to listen to you speak for one minute. Do you make any of those useless additions? Possibly not, if you are monitoring yourself. Extend the period of time you are speaking. Are there any additions, stammering, or repetitions now?

Many speech "problems" are really just bad habits.

Your goal, of course, is to eliminate all unnecessary words or sounds, no matter what the length of time. If you can't achieve that when only a friend is listening, imagine the difficulty you'll have when someone important is within earshot. In fact, the pressure of speaking when it "matters" is often what triggers those offending extras.

✍ EXERCISE

Ask a friend to listen to your speech habits. Have your friend ask you a few easy questions, such as those that follow. Answer the questions as naturally as possible, and have your friend note your sentence structure, body language, clarity, and use of stalling words such as "ummm" and "ahhh." After your friend has shared his or her notes with you, try answering the same questions again, this time correcting any mistakes you have made.

- How was your day?
- What is your favorite sport?
- Who is someone you look up to and why?
- Where would you most like to live in the world?
- When is your favorite time of year?

Nervous gestures, such as touching your face or hair, wringing your hands, and other kinds of fidgeting, should also be avoided. When a confident presence is called for, nervous habits give us away.

Another annoying habit is speaking too fast. Again, this often is only a problem when you are under pressure. Most people talk faster when they are nervous. But if your normal conversational tempo is speedy, practice slowing down. Talking too fast can come across as flippant or even evasive.

LISTEN UP! TIPS FOR LISTENING EFFECTIVELY

- Look at whoever is speaking and give that person your full attention.

- Take notes if necessary.

- Always let the other person finish a sentence or train of thought.

- Ask questions to clarify points that you may not understand completely.

- Summarize what the other person has said in your own words to show that you are on the same page.

Slang may also be regarded as flippant. Take care to limit slang to words you hear your superiors commonly using. Foul language, on the other hand, has no place in the workplace. Never curse, even if you hear a superior curse continually.

LEARNING LEADERSHIP ON THE JOB

Since all leadership positions involve working with others, consider your coworkers training ground for practicing leadership skills. Be willing to run the meeting, if it's all the same to them. But don't be too aggressive or lecture your coworkers. Learn to listen and observe rather than talk too much. Leaders know that the more you talk, the less others listen. Listening has the added benefit of helping you become better informed. When you do speak, you will have something intelligent to say.

ROLE MODELS

One way to learn leadership skills is by studying them in others and modeling your behavior on theirs. A person you respect and admire can become your *role model*. The skills he or she exhibits as a leader make him or her a person after whom you want to model yourself. *Reverse role models* can teach us how not to do something. Choosing a role model is serious business.

DID YOU KNOW?

A survey by Harris Interactive on behalf of Junior Achievement found that 64 percent of teenagers had a role model. Teens reported that they wanted their role models to care about others, not be afraid of failure, and be interested in making a positive contribution to society through his or her business practices.

"I know I have a lot to learn. I'm still a baby in this business," says Lindsay. "But I'm willing to learn. Some of my peers kind of teased me for being so quiet

✍ EXERCISE

- Think about role models that you have observed in work situations. Write down how a positive role model has helped you to learn how to work effectively.

- Then think of a negative role model you have encountered—one who showed you how not to do something. Write down what he or she said or did that made you not want to model your own behavior similarly.

when I first started here. But I figured if I didn't have something useful to say, I'd be better off just listening. At meetings, I noticed which people seemed to have the respect of the management. I watched how they acted—none of them were big talkers either. But when they did speak, people listened."

Lindsay adds, "In my department, one woman in particular impressed me. I began to pay attention to how she handled things, what kind of assignments she volunteered for, and so on. I learned some really helpful ways of dealing with coworkers just by watching her. She recently got a well-deserved promotion to another department. I miss having her close by. Even though I'm more sure of myself now, I'm on the lookout for a new role model."

No matter how much we think we know, there is always more to learn. If you want to learn how to lead, select a role model that others respect and follow.

MENTORS

Sometimes the role models you choose are not even aware you are modeling your behavior on theirs. In other cases, a role model may offer to show you the ropes. This person will take a more direct interest in your needs and offer his or her experience to help you in your career. This individual, called a *mentor,* will be a wise adviser and counselor.

A mentor knows what you need to do to reach your goals and can teach you what you need to know to get ahead in your field. Besides imparting actual know-how to help you do your job, a mentor will share his or her experienced view of how your company works. This person will tutor you in the ways of the business world. A mentor is like a coach, encouraging you, pushing you, and showing you ways to be more effective. And the best mentor is also a promoter. He or she will be your champion within the company, making sure that you have opportunities to learn and grow.

In certain contexts you won't have to look for a mentor: Sometimes a mentor will find you. Some companies have formalized mentoring programs. They automatically assign senior employees to mentor younger, less-experienced workers. These companies

A mentor (far left) *observes a first-year teacher as she works with students. A mentor can help you reach your goals and teach you the ins and outs of your job.* (Tracy Boulian, The Plain Dealer/AP Photo)

realize the value of supporting and developing those who will be the company's future leaders.

Here are a few examples of the mentorship programs offered by major companies:

- McGraw-Hill, an information media company, pairs mentors and middle-to-upper-level mentees from different business areas to encourage cross-segment collaboration and learning.

- Each year, the auto giant General Motors selects 20 of its top female employees to participate in cross-company mentoring.

Upon completion of the program, 94 percent of mentees reported an improvement in their ability to think strategically and 88 percent reported improved leadership skills and their ability to meet workplace challenges.

- New engineers at General Dynamics General Boat, a manufacturer of submarines for the U.S. navy, are paired with an experienced mentor. They work together on the mentor's projects, which gradually become larger and more involved as the mentee gains experience. Mentees eventually take over some of their mentor's projects or receive new assignments that they tackle on their own.

- Thomson Reuters, an information media company, offers a mentoring program that seeks to encourage high-performing staff to improve their understanding of diversity issues and impart these lessons to other employees.

- Intel, a major computer hardware and software manufacturer, offers several mentoring programs, including one that matches mentors and mentees by specific in-demand skills, not by years of experience or job title. Mentees, known as "partners" at Intel, enter their interests into a computer database, which generates possible mentor matches. Intel creates accountability by asking participants to sign a nonbinding contract that encourages them to continue to participate in the program, which is open to anyone—from line workers to senior-level engineers.

Everyone will benefit from having a mentor, but for anyone interested in leadership in a company, a mentor is essential. So don't wait indefinitely to be "found." Be willing to take the initiative and find your own mentor through the following steps:

1. Consider your abilities objectively. What skills do you have and where do you think they will take you in your company?

2. Observe who has knowledge and influence in that area.

3. Approach a senior employee whose business style seems similar to your own. Let this individual know what your interests and goals are and that you welcome his or her advice and counsel. If this person seems willing to be a resource for you, you may be on your way to a mentor relationship.

Ideally, every boss is a mentor to some extent. It is certainly in your boss's best interest that you

SURF THE WEB: FINDING A MENTOR

MentorNet: The E-Mentoring Network for Diversity in Engineering and Science
   http://www.mentornet.net

MENTOR/National Mentoring Partnership
   http://www.mentoring.org

Professional Coaches and Mentors Association
   http://www.pcmaonline.com

perform well in your job. But mentoring also involves helping you become more visible in your company, and not every boss is in a position or has the desire to do this. The staff of Catalyst, in their book *Making the Most of Your First Job,* cite numerous successful relationships in which a boss is also a mentor. However, they caution, "Don't try to force your boss into becoming your mentor if the willingness isn't there. It may be that your boss feels uneasy singling you out as his or her protégé over your coworkers. Or perhaps your career ambitions conflict with your boss's. Whatever the reason, if you sense reluctance on the part of your boss, search for your mentor in the ranks of higher management or in another department."

FEMALE LEADERS FACE SPECIAL WORKPLACE CHALLENGES

Although women have made many strides in the workplace, there is still a glass ceiling in many industries that keeps many qualified women from advancing to top management positions. Catalyst, a nonprofit research and advocacy organization for women, conducts an annual census that tracks the status of women in leadership positions. In 2008, it found that although women make up 46.3 percent of the labor force, they make up only 15.7 percent of Fortune 500 corporate officers, hold only 15.1 percent of seats on the boards of Fortune 500 companies, and make up only 2.4 percent of Fortune 500 CEOs.

Female managers often face a double standard in the workplace. If they demonstrate leadership qualities that are typically associated with men, they are considered too hard or demanding. If they demonstrate qualities that are typically labeled as stereotypically female, they are considered soft and not able to effectively do their jobs. They also often earn lower pay than men for the same level and quality of work and may be sexually harassed by coworkers.

In recent years, companies have taken major steps to improve gender diversity by instituting zero-tolerance policies for sexual harassment, increasing pay for women, and implementing managerial training programs for promising female employees. Some companies—such as American Express, FedEx,

A female executive at a textile factory reviews inventory
with a manager. Despite recent gains, women are still vastly
underrepresented at the executive level at Fortune 500 companies.
(Jim Craigmyle, Corbis)

Grant Thornton, KPMG, Manpower, MetLife, Turner
Broadcasting, and UPS—have been lauded by women's
groups and magazines for becoming industry leaders
in promoting gender diversity.

So if you're a young woman, how do you
break through the glass ceiling? Here are a few
suggestions:

- Take advantage of any women-oriented
  management-training programs offered by
  your company.

- Find a female mentor or role model who
  can help you advance at your company.

- Join professional associations that are geared toward women.

- If you are still searching for a job, try to learn more about companies that are known for being female-friendly.

- Never stand for any form of sexual harassment in the workplace.

- Always work hard and be yourself! It will eventually pay off.

MAKE AND TAKE OPPORTUNITIES

While you are looking for role models and mentors, there are also things you can do on your own to develop leadership skills. As mentioned earlier, positive interaction with your coworkers is essential. If you have a relationship of mutual trust with your peers, they will tell you their honest opinion of your endeavors—and possibly those of anyone else in the company! In *On Leadership*, John W. Gardner focuses on the value of truly knowing your coworkers when he says, "If [young people] are to be leaders, they must come to learn how other workers feel about their jobs, how they regard those above them in the hierarchy, what motivates them, what lifts their morale, and what lowers it. For all of that, the workplace is a learning laboratory."

The workplace is also where you will learn the practical side of your business. Unlike school

READ MORE ABOUT IT: FEMALE LEADERS

Barry, Kathleen. *Susan B. Anthony: A Biography of a Singular Feminist.* Rev. ed. Bloomington, Ind.: 1st Books Library, 2000.

Berlinski, Claire. *There Is No Alternative: Why Margaret Thatcher Matters.* New York: Basic Books, 2008.

Bernstein, Carl. *A Woman in Charge: The Life of Hillary Rodham Clinton.* New York: Vintage Books, 2008.

Burkett, Elinor. *Golda.* New York: Harper, 2008.

Fiorina, Carly. *Tough Choices: A Memoir.* New York: Portfolio Trade, 2007.

Harris, Cynthia M. *Eleanor Roosevelt: A Biography.* Westport, Conn.: Greenwood Press, 2007.

Keller, Emily. *Frances Perkins: First Woman Cabinet Member.* Greensboro, N.C.: Morgan Reynolds Publishing, 2006.

Pelosi, Nancy, and Amy Hill Hearth. *Know Your Power: A Message to America's Daughters.* New York: Doubleday, 2008.

assignments, which usually ask you to practice something you have already been taught, work assignments often require you to learn something new in order to solve a problem. Since problem solving is an important ability for leadership, a mentor steers you into these desirable assignments. If you don't have a mentor, try to get as great a variety of assignments as possible. You may even want to volunteer to take on an assignment from another department.

The organization concerned to develop its young potential leaders reassigns them periodically with a view to posing new challenges, testing new skills, and introducing them to new constituencies.

—John W. Gardner, *On Leadership*

One way to build a constituency, or following, is to volunteer to lead a committee. If this opportunity does not present itself at work, you may want to seek a community-service leadership position. Just remember that no one likes a dictator. In Gardner's words, people like the leader to play a "first among equals" role.

Another way to attract followers is to become an expert at a particular task or procedure—and always be willing to help others with it. This does not mean that you must become narrow in your interests and abilities. In fact, a leader needs to become a generalist: one who has knowledge of many aspects of an organization's operation.

People like the leader to play a "first among equals" role.

*Make yourself a resource who people rely on and can
go to for questions, information, special expertise, or
access to information.*

—**Bradley G. Richardson** in *Jobsmarts
for Twentysomethings*

TRAINING PROGRAMS

Many companies have training programs to develop
leadership skills. A survey in *Training Magazine* (http://
www.trainingmag.com) shows that 64 percent of
U.S. companies with 100 or more employees provide some type of training in areas related to leadership. Of these companies, 69 percent offer training
specifically in leadership skills, 61 percent in team
building, 59 percent in listening skills, and 53 percent in problem solving.

Some companies conduct periodic appraisal inter-
views. These evaluations should not only assess the
employee's abilities and achievements, but provide
specific recommendations for future improvement.
Companies that do not specifically rate leadership
abilities usually evaluate related categories such as
getting along with peers and communication skills.

LEADERSHIP DEVELOPMENT

The development of leadership ability follows many
paths, but it begins with self-awareness. You can help

COMPANIES WITH
TOP TRAINING PROGRAMS

Company	Comment
1. General Electric	Has legendary U.S. training facility, which has now been expanded to overseas locations. Also known for its online leadership workshops.
2. Procter & Gamble	Recruiters seek applicants with leadership ability who have an "in-touch capability."
3. Nokia	Has innovative mentorship program and asks subordinates to rate leadership and training qualities of top 200 executives in company.
4. Hindustan Unilever	Managers are ranked by color; top managers (green, as in "go") are fast-tracked into company-critical positions.
5. Capital One Financial	Newly hired managers are paired with "personal trainers," who help them develop their leadership skills.
6. General Mills	Offers a simulation program to help employees address unexpected workplace challenges.
7. McKinsey	With offices in 45 countries, McKinsey offers a program that allows employees to work for 12 to 24 months in two foreign countries.
8. IBM	Has created a work group of 300 senior executives to improve its leadership base.
9. BBVA	Workers who are designated for promotion are not only assessed by their bosses, but also by their coworkers. BBVA believes this process reveals workers with a participatory approach to leadership.
10. Infosys Technologies	Has implemented a program called Voice For Youth, in which twentysomething employees are given a seat on its management council.

Source: *Fortune*, October 1, 2007

yourself learn to lead by viewing your talents and image objectively and by observing and imitating the leadership qualities of role models and mentors.

But ultimately, leadership is about awareness of others—those you aspire to lead. You must be sensitive to the feelings and needs of those who are to follow you. Build your team based on mutual trust and respect. Offer positive feedback as well as constructive criticism; be willing to learn from subordinates as well as superiors. A leader cannot truly succeed without the support of those he or she leads.

Ultimately, leadership is about awareness of others—those you aspire to lead.

SKILLS FOR FUTURE LEADERS

In 2007, the Center for Creative Leadership conducted a survey of business leaders to determine trends in leadership. Some of the most interesting findings include:

- Seventy-six percent of respondents believed that the "definition of effective leadership had changed in the past five years."

- More than 91 percent of respondents believed that leaders face more complex challenges than they did in the past. The top factors fueling these challenges included "internal changes to the organization, market dynamics, a shortage of talent, and globalization."

Continued on page 136

Continued from page 135

- Ninety-seven percent of senior managers felt that collaboration was a key to workplace success, but only 47 percent of these leaders believed leaders at their companies actually had this skill.

- Sixty-five percent of respondents predicted that there would be a shortage of middle and top leaders in coming years. The report found that "organizations will need to find innovative ways to...meet the development and career needs of those just entering the workforce."

- Managers reported that the most significant trend that they saw emerging in leadership was the shift from an autocratic leadership style to one that is more participative. Leaders predicted that future leaders would need to "depend on the ability to be collaborative and to focus on the team rather than the individual."

✔ TRUE OR FALSE: ANSWERS

Are You Ready to Lead?

1. Personal appearance matters in the workplace—especially for managers.

True. By dressing to match your corporate culture, you send a message to your employees that you're professional and that you're on board with your company's goals and objectives. It may even help you get promoted. Ninety-three percent of managers surveyed by OfficeTeam said that a worker's style of dress "somewhat" or "significantly" influenced their chances of being promoted.

2. I can wear anything I want on Casual Friday.

False. Company policies vary, so check with your boss before deciding to wear your favorite jeans and concert T-shirt on Casual Friday. For more information, see Surf the Web: What to Wear-Business Casual on page 112.

3. Successful leaders don't just issue orders: They lead by example.

True. This ranges from arriving to work on time and following new company dress codes, to getting your hands dirty by helping out on projects and other tasks.

4. Mentors are more experienced coworkers who offer to show you the ropes on the job.

True. A good mentor knows what you need to do to reach your goals, can teach you how to get ahead in your career, and will always have your best interests at heart.

IN SUMMARY . . .

- Appearance can make or break a first impression. Observe what your classmates, coworkers, or team members wear; dress accordingly.

- Leaders show their personality and ability in their actions and words, not simply in their appearance.

- Your attitude can be seen in your body language, so make sure your actions and movements convey the right message.

- Effective speaking and listening habits can be developed through practice and conscious effort.

- Role models and mentors should be used to model your behavior and to strive to be a better person, worker, classmate, etc.

- Leaders should always want to learn and improve their abilities.

- Leaders are always aware of and sensitive to others.

WEB SITES

Body Language

Answers.com: Body Language
http://www.answers.com/topic/body-language

Gestures: Body Language and Nonverbal
Communication
http://www.csupomona.edu/~tassi/gestures.
htm#gestures

What the Boss' Body Language Says
http://hotjobs.yahoo.com/career-articles-what_
the_boss_body_language_says-306

Charts

Brief Tutorial on Gantt Charts
http://www.me.umn.edu/courses/me4054/
assignments/gantt.html

Flowcharting Help Page
http://home.att.net/~dexter.a.hansen/flowchart/
flowchart.htm

Gantt Chart
  http://www.ganttchart.com

Gliffy: Flow Charts
  http://www.gliffy.com/free-flow-chart-software

Inc.com: Flow Charts
  http://www.inc.com/encyclopedia/flow-charts.
  html

Mind Tools: Flow Charts
  http://www.mindtools.com/pages/article/
  newTMC_97.htm

What Is a Gantt Chart?
  http://www.brighthub.com/office/project-
  management/articles/6550.aspx

Communication Skills

Free Management Library: Communications Skills
  http://www.managementhelp.org/commskls/
  cmm_face.htm

Decision Making

Decision Making
  http://www.decisionmaking.org

Dress, Office

About.com: Business Casual Dress Code
  http://humanresources.about.com/od/
  glossaryd/g/dress_code.htm

Business Casual Attire
http://www.career.vt.edu/JOBSEARC/BusCasual.htm

How to Dress Business Casual—Men
http://www.ehow.com/how_41_dress-business-casual.html

How to Dress Business Casual—Women
http://www.ehow.com/how_49_dress-business-casual.html

Ethics

Center for Ethical Business Cultures
http://www.cebcglobal.org

Ethics Resource Center
http://www.ethics.org

LeaderValues.com
http://www.leader-values.com

General

American Management Association
http://www.amanet.org

Center for Creative Leadership
http://www.ccl.org

Junior Achievement
http://www.ja.org

Leadership Styles
http://www.nwlink.com/~donclark/leader/leadstl.html

Leadership Style Survey Quiz
http://www.nwlink.com/~donclark/leader/
survstyl.html

MindTools
http://www.mindtools.com

Motivation and Leadership Styles
http://www.motivation-tools.com/workplace/
leadership_styles.htm

NMA . . . The Leadership Development Association
http://nma1.org

National Outdoor Leadership School
http://www.nols.edu

O*NET OnLine
http://online.onetcenter.org

Work911.com
http://www.work911.com

Meetings

EffectiveMeetings.com
http://www.effectivemeetings.com

Meeting Wizard
http://www.meetingwizard.com

Mentors

MENTOR/National Mentoring Partnership
http://www.mentoring.org

MentorNet: The E-Mentoring Network for Diversity
in Engineering and Science
http://www.mentornet.net

Mind Tools: Running Effective Meetings
http://www.mindtools.com/CommSkll/
RunningMeetings.htm

Professional Coaches and Mentors Association
http://www.pcmaonline.com

Work911.com: Effective Meetings
http://www.work911.com/articles/meetmgt.
htm

Teamwork

Manual for Working in Teams
http://www.analytictech.com/mb021/teamhint.
htm

Surviving the Group Project: A Note on Working in
Teams
http://web.cba.neu.edu/~ewertheim/teams/
ovrvw2.htm#Introduction

Team Building
http://www.meetingwizard.org/meetings/team-
building.cfm

13 Ways to Encourage Teamwork
http://www.askmen.com/money/
successful_100/115_success.html

Women

Catalyst
http://www.catalyst.org

Worldwide Guide to Women in Leadership
http://www.guide2womenleaders.com

GLOSSARY

accountability willingness to accept responsibility

adequate sufficient; enough to meet the required needs of a situation

assessment determination of the value or worth of something, often a property

authoritarian leadership style a management style in which the leader assigns tasks with little or no input from employees

autocratic leadership style See **authoritarian leadership style**

body language nonverbal communication composed of gestures or movements

business casual a more relaxed office dress code that replaces the traditional business suit with more casual attire (khaki pants, cotton shirts, etc.); the extent of how casual workers may dress is up to the discretion of the individual business

charismatic leadership style a management style in which the leader uses energetic encouragement to inspire his or her teams

confrontation a meeting of two or more parties with clashing interests or ideas

constituency a following or group of supporters

constructive criticism polite and useful suggestions that can help improve an individual's work

constructively competitive being competitive without alienating others; competition that is helpful toward achieving the final goal

deadline a required date or time by which work must be completed

delegate to assign tasks or responsibilities to another individual

delegative leadership style a management style in which the leader lets the members of his or her work group make most or all decisions and provides little or no guidance

democratic leadership style See **participative leadership style**

ethics a system or morals; the code of rules about how we act toward others

feedback opinions of others on a person's performance

flow chart chart showing each task of a project in sequence

free reign leadership style See **delegative leadership style**

Gantt chart chart showing the timing of both simultaneous and sequential tasks and the relative amount of time allotted for each

glass ceiling a situation in which workers cannot advance to higher levels due to discrimination

goal the desired end toward which work is directed

mentor a wise adviser

morale positive feelings toward a team and its effort

motivation the process of encouraging individuals or groups to act

multitask consisting of many tasks

notebook tracking using a notebook to track the progress of a project or task

overmanaging managing a team or individual to an excessive degree; usually detrimental to the group or individual's effort

participative leadership style a management style in which the leader encourages suggestions from his or her workers and participates in group assignments to encourage team spirit

performance review a formal meeting in which a manager provides feedback to a worker about his or her job performance

priorities tasks, people, or events that are given attention before other alternatives

progress check monitoring the pace and quality of a team's work

promotion the act of raising an individual to an elevated stature or position

purchase order (P.O.) a document or form required for the buying of goods or services

reverse role model an individual who has the opposite effect of a role model; someone whose behavior you do not want to imitate

role model a person whose behavior is observed and imitated

sensitivity an awareness of the needs and feelings of others

simultaneous actions happening at the same time

situational leadership style a management style in which leaders switch back and forth between leadership styles based on the project requirements and the personalities of their employees

social skills the ability to interact with others

street smarts the opposite of book smarts; knowledge not gained through reading or lectures, but through experience

tasks-by-levels chart chart in which tasks are divided by levels and put into columns

timetable schedule showing the planned time of event occurrence or task completion

time/task analysis chart See **Gantt chart**

transformational leadership style a management style in which the leader possesses extraordinary inspirational skills to encourage his or her employees to meet goals

two-way feedback the exchange of ideas between two groups or individuals

unwritten rules required behavior that is expected but not stated in any manual, meeting, etc.; rules that are expected to be followed by others in an organization or common group

BIBLIOGRAPHY

Allen, David. *Getting Things Done: The Art of Stress-Free Productivity*. New York: Penguin Books, 2002.

———. *Ready for Anything: 52 Productivity Principles for Work and Life*. New York: Penguin Books, 2004.

Andersen, Peter. *The Complete Idiot's Guide to Body Language*. New York: Alpha, 2004.

Badaracco, Joseph. *Defining Moments: When Managers Must Choose Between Right and Right*. Cambridge, Mass.: Harvard Business School Press, 1997.

Barry, Kathleen. *Susan B. Anthony: A Biography of a Singular Feminist*. Rev. ed. Bloomington, Ind.: 1st Books Library, 2000.

Berlinski, Claire. *There Is No Alternative: Why Margaret Thatcher Matters*. New York: Basic Books, 2008.

Bernstein, Carl. *A Woman in Charge: The Life of Hillary Rodham Clinton*. New York: Vintage Books, 2008.

Burkett, Elinor. *Golda*. New York: Harper, 2008.

Ciampa, Dan, and Michael Watkins. *Right From The Start: Taking Charge in a New Leadership Role.* Boston, Mass.: Harvard Business School Press, 2005.

Covey, Sean. *The 7 Habits of Highly Effective Teens.* New York: Fireside Press, 1998.

Covey, Stephen R. *The 7 Habits of Highly Effective People.* 15th ed. New York: The Free Press, 2004.

CultureGrams 2009 World Edition. Ann Arbor, Mich.: Proquest LLC, 2008.

Dresser, Norine. *Multicultural Manners: Essential Rules of Etiquette for the 21st Century.* Rev. ed. Hoboken, N.J.: Wiley, 2005.

Evans, Clare. *Time Management for Dummies.* Hoboken, N.J.: For Dummies, 2008.

Fiorina, Carly. *Tough Choices: A Memoir.* New York: Portfolio Trade, 2007.

Fisher, Roger, and Alan Sharp. *Getting It Done: How to Lead When You're Not in Charge.* New York: Collins Business, 1999.

Fournies, Ferdinand. *Why Employees Don't Do What They're Supposed To and What You Can Do About It.* 2d ed. New York: McGraw-Hill, 2007.

Fox, Sue. *Etiquette for Dummies.* 2d ed. Hoboken, N.J.: For Dummies, 2007.

Goldberg, Jan. *Careers for Extroverts & Other Gregarious Types.* 2d ed. New York: McGraw-Hill, 2005.

Gunther, Robert E., Stephen J. Hoch, and Howard C. Kunreuther. *Wharton on Making Decisions.* Hoboken, N.J.: Wiley, 2004.

Hammond, John S., Ralph L. Keeney, and Howard Raiffa. *Smart Choices: A Practical Guide to Making Better Decisions.* New York: Broadway Books, 2002.

Harris, Cynthia M. *Eleanor Roosevelt: A Biography.* Westport, Conn.: Greenwood Press, 2007.

Harvey, Andrew J., and Raymond E. Foster. *Leadership: Texas Hold 'Em Style.* Charleston, S.C.: BookSurge, 2007.

Henderson, David R., Charles L. Hooper, and Mark Lawler. *Making Great Decisions in Business and Life.* Chicago Park, Calif.: Chicago Park Press, 2007.

Henderson, Veronique, and Pat Henshaw. *Image Matters for Men: How to Dress for Success!* London, U.K.: Hamlyn, 2007.

Hollender, Jeffrey. *What Matters Most: How a Small Group of Pioneers Is Teaching Social Responsibility to Big Business, and Why Big Business Is Listening.* New York: Basic Books, 2006.

Idowu, Samuel O., and Walter Leal Filho. *Global Practices of Corporate Social Responsibility.* New York: Springer Publishing Company, 2008.

Jackson, John, and Lorraine Bosse-Smith. *Leveraging Your Leadership Style: Maximize Your Influence by*

Discovering the Leader Within. Nashville, Tenn.: Abingdon Press, 2008.

Kahane, Adam. *Solving Tough Problems: An Open Way of Talking, Listening, and Creating New Realities*. 2d ed. San Francisco: Berrett-Koehler Publishers, 2007.

Karson, Jill. *Profiles in History: Leaders of the Civil Rights Movement*. Farmington Hills, Mich.: Greenhaven Press, 2004.

Keller, Emily. *Frances Perkins: First Woman Cabinet Member*. Greensboro, N.C.: Morgan Reynolds Publishing, 2006.

Klaus, Peggy. *The Hard Truth About Soft Skills: Workplace Lessons Smart People Wish They'd Learned Sooner*. New York: Collins Business, 2008.

Kolb, Robert W. *Encyclopedia of Business Ethics and Society*. Thousand Oaks, Calif.: Sage Publications, 2007.

Lenius, Oscar. *A Well-Dressed Gentleman's Pocket Guide*. London, U.K.: Prion, 2006.

Lerner, Dick. *Dress Like the Big Fish: How to Achieve the Image You Want and the Success You Deserve*. Omaha, Neb.: Bel Air Fashions Press, 2008.

Lodge, Tom. *Mandela: A Critical Life*. New York: Oxford University Press, USA, 2007.

MacKinnon, Barbara. *Ethics: Theory and Contemporary Issues*. 6th ed. Florence, Ky.: Wadsworth Publishing, 2008.

Maxwell, John C. *Developing the Leader Within You.* Nashville, Tenn.: Thomas Nelson, 2005.

———. *The 21 Indispensable Qualities of a Leader: Becoming the Person Others Will Want to Follow.* 2d ed. Nashville, Tenn.: Thomas Nelson, 2007.

———. *The 21 Irrefutable Laws of Leadership: Follow Them and People Will Follow You.* Rev. ed. Nashville, Tenn.: Thomas Nelson, 2007.

McCain, John, and Mark Salter. *Faith of My Fathers: A Family Memoir.* New York: Harper, 2008.

Miller, Patrick W. *Body Language on the Job.* Munster, Ind.: Patrick W. Miller & Associates, 2006.

Obama, Barack. *Dreams from My Father: A Story of Race and Inheritance.* New York: Three Rivers Press, 2004.

Pelosi, Nancy, and Amy Hill Hearth. *Know Your Power: A Message to America's Daughters.* New York: Doubleday, 2008.

Peres, Daniel. *Details Men's Style Manual: The Ultimate Guide for Making Your Clothes Work for You.* New York: Gotham, 2007.

Peters, Thomas J., and Robert H. Waterman. *In Search of Excellence: Lessons from America's Best-Run Companies.* New York: Collins Business, 2004.

Potter, Ronald, and Wayne Hastings. *Trust Me: Developing a Leadership Style People Will Follow.* Charleston, S.C.: BookSurge, 2008.

Reiman, Tonya. *The Power of Body Language.* New York: Pocket, 2007.

Thiroux, Jacques P., and Keith W. Krasemann. *Ethics: Theory and Practice.* 9th ed. Upper Saddle River, N.J.: Prentice Hall, 2006.

Weigel, George. *Witness to Hope: The Biography of Pope John Paul II.* New York: Harper Perennial, 2005.

Weingarten, Rachel C. *Career and Corporate Cool.* Hoboken, N.J.: Wiley, 2007.

Index